POWER SABBATICAL

POWER SABBATICAL

The Break That Makes a Difference

Robert Scott Levine

FINDHORN
Press

First published by Findhorn Press 2007

ISBN: 978-1-84409-096-9

Edited by Magaer Lennox
Cover design by Damian Keenan
Layout by Pam Bochel
Printed and bound in the USA

1 2 3 4 5 6 7 8 9 10 11 12 13 12 11 10 09 08 07 06

Published by
Findhorn Press
305A The Park,
Findhorn, Forres
Scotland IV36 3TE

Tel 01309 690582
Fax 01309 690036
email: info@findhornpress.com
www.findhornpress.com

Contents

1 : Introduction

1.1 The dream and the reality

Millions admit dreaming of taking an extended period of leave from their work and lives. On top of that, millions of others suffer from job-related stress, feelings of "disconnection" with community and society, and other dissatisfaction with their lives but may not yet be aware that a sabbatical can help. It is easy to accept that the importance of maintaining balance between work and personal life, and periodically "renewing" one's self, is one of the most valued principles of any advanced society. We know that youth and health are fleeting, and that we cannot wind back the clock on things left undone. Even in the hard-driving, capitalist American society, recent college graduates and new workers have said that behind compensation, work-life balance is their biggest career concern, according to the Society for Human Resource Management.

So how many people actually want extended leave or sabbaticals? A 2001 survey quoted by *American Demographics* found that more than 60% of Generation X employees want one. A survey that same year by New York-based nonprofit Catalyst revealed similar results: 18% of Generation X workers currently take extended leave and sabbaticals, and an additional 43% would like to. According to a 2001 survey by The Principal Financial Group, more than half the employees of small and midsized companies say they long for a sabbatical. And a more recent survey from a recruitment consultancy found that almost half of all office workers would take a sabbatical if they could. This is not just a U.S. phenomenon. Three-quarters of those surveyed by British-based Direct Line Travel Insurance said they would consider taking a long break, and according to their estimates 6.2 million professionals have already left their day jobs for months at a time to travel, spend time with family, or further their education.

But how many of these people have then rejected the idea of a sabbatical because of fear, money, or family considerations? How many more have never even thought about it in the first place –

though they may be excellent candidates for one? It is impossible to say, but let's explore this some more. While searches at the major online booksellers return thousands of results for the categories of "work-life balance," "job stress," and "career planning," a search for "sabbatical" non-fiction works normally returns less than fifteen in-print books. This suggests that people are searching for solutions to problems, but haven't thought about a sabbatical as one of them. I hope to show you the positive changes a sabbatical can bring and show you how practical a sabbatical can truly be.

In fact, I plan to show you how it can make sense to quit a decent-paying job to take a year off to travel, study, or relax. Even if you were just laid off, you should consider taking an extended leave of absence from work before hitting the jobs section in the ads! And when you're overstressed, burnt out, and fatigued, do you really think a two-week vacation will do the trick for very long?

The distressing reality is that the workplace is less and less friendly to your needs as an individual, as a person. Layoffs, outsourcing, global competition, bigger workloads, longer days, and the like increase the pressure on all workers to perform at the expense of their personal lives. There are over 10 million unemployed Americans with at least 0.5 million of these due to job outsourcing; this number excludes the scores of unemployed who become ineligible for unemployment benefits every week and therefore are no longer even counted among the unemployed.

And "older" workers are all the more vulnerable to job loss and outsourcing. The U.S. Bureau of Labor Statistics paints an especially bleak picture for 55 to 64 year-old workers, who are up to 69% less likely to find new jobs once displaced from the workforce than younger workers (many end up taking much lower paying jobs, and 20% just drop out of the workforce entirely). One set of numbers quoted in the book *Outsourcing America: What's Behind Our National Crisis and How We Can Reclaim American Jobs*[1] indicated that of those in the 55–64 year-old age bracket, who lost their jobs from 2001–2003 only 65% were rehired, and 57% of them took a pay cut from their previous position. An article in the May 2005 issue of *Fortune* magazine, a survey of human resource (HR) managers taken by the Society for Human Resource Management indicates that 53% of them felt that older workers did not keep up with technology, and 28% felt that they were less flexible. This issue also quotes evidence that suggests that "older" workers that are involuntarily displaced are less likely to reenter the workforce.

There's more. Technological advancement has made us reachable wherever we go – increasing productivity to an even greater detriment to our shrinking personal time. Despite the promise of these measures to better balance work and personal life, these "work-life" innovations like ', shortened workweeks, and telecommuting have not been widely adopted. So let's see the challenge for what it is: how do we reclaim our time for ourselves?

The fact is, many people don't think about a sabbatical or extended leave of absence from work and daily life as something even worth considering! Sure, it sounds like a great idea. For many of us, it is only on long airplane journeys or during that all-too-short vacation that we see our lives for what they've become – and dream of what they might yet be.

"My doctor says that stress may kill me. And it's no secret why. I don't smoke or drink, exercise regularly, and I eat right – I just work 65 hours a week and don't know how I can scale back. I feel trapped in a train heading for a collision. What do I do?"

"My job isn't so bad, but…I am so sick of doing the same thing, day in and day out. My boss is a moron and I can't relate to my co-workers. I know I need to make a change but don't know what to change or how."

"I feel so disconnected. I'm not part of my community and am so tired that I haven't been to religious services at all lately. At work, everyone deals with me only because they have to, because they need something from me. I want to feel like I'm really needed, making a difference, and helping people."

"If I had the time, I would explore the jungles of Brazil."

"I'd much rather own and cook for a small restaurant than work as an accountant."

"My family seems to be growing apart. Wouldn't it be fantastic if we could actually spend time with one another, and not just in our own separate lives?"

In fact a sabbatical can be one of the best ways to face these challenges by allowing you to reclaim your time for your own needs. Sabbaticals can and should be used to de-stress and detoxify your life. You can spend all or part of a sabbatical reflecting, contemplating, and planning the next phases of your life. This book will show you how to take a "power sabbatical" by defining *your* needs, then planning how to meet these needs during – and after – the sabbatical. The planning system I will explain works whether your needs are oriented towards family, community, spirituality, career or creative development, or other personal interests. And it even works if you are not sure what your needs really are; just that some void in your life needs to be filled... Taking a sabbatical can also be surprisingly affordable using established financial and tax-planning methods in concert with the planning tools presented in this book.

1.2 The search for guidance

I have a confession to make. I am not a work-life guru, nor have I conducted academic-quality research on the scores of people who have taken sabbaticals (though I have taken one myself). I have, before seeking growth and balance through my own sabbatical, researched just about everything about sabbaticals that I could get my hands on, and talked to as many people as I could who already had taken or at least had seriously considered them. I then applied the project-planning and risk-management skills I use every day as a consultant, and the practical experiences I'd gained traveling to and living in many lands, to sabbatical planning. As a project manager, I was struck by the similarities in planning for and executing large, complex projects and planning a sabbatical. Later, I realized that this is exactly what a sabbatical is. I also saw synergy in crafting a winning sales proposal (a survival skill for us consultants) and writing a sabbatical proposal. Finally, the art of managing risks in a project is easily transferable to managing risks in your sabbatical plan. We will see how effective we can be when we use project-management guidelines to help plan a successful sabbatical.

I believed in the promise of a sabbatical myself, and put my own plan to the test when I quit my high-paying, high-pressure career as a business consultant to experience a sabbatical with my family in another country, to learn more about our heritage, and to de-stress. I scoured the bookstores looking for help in preparing for a sabbatical but found only limited and generic information. Some titles suggested that sabbaticals are most appropriate for academics, clergy, or the wealthy. Others seemed to assume that only adventure-travelers took sabbaticals (believe it or not, taking off a year to care for mom and finish that graduate degree can also be a satisfying sabbatical). Most other books operated from the assumption that if you are not wealthy, you must therefore seek sponsorship from your employer, as professors and priests do. That alone helps us to understand why more people have not turned the dream of a sabbatical into a reality – so few enterprises actually offer meaningful sabbatical programs for their employees. Further, more and more workers are actually contractors or temporary workers not covered by such programs even if they did exist. Finally, every sabbatical book had one thing in common: anecdotes in place of advice, random tips thrown about that may or may not apply to your situation, and lists of resources that were narrowly focused and very likely out of date a few years after the book was published.

My next stop was the career and financial-planning section of the bookstore. I didn't expect that these books would pay much mind to the positive spiritual, health, and other life benefits of a sabbatical – I was just curious whether planning for an extended break was at all touched upon. In fact, I still haven't located a book that speaks to the positive impact of a focused and extended break on long-term financial health. One would imagine these books calculating the costs of lost income and the expenses of a sabbatical against the difficult-to-estimate (though very much real) benefits of a sabbatical. Yet such a profit-loss approach is flawed, since the financial benefits of a power sabbatical are not always easily quantified, especially in the short term. This view also ignores the long-term damage to career and finances that can be caused by burnout and stress (lost working time, increased medical costs), by flagging creativity and skills (lower income, passed-up promotions), and by lost income due to opportunities never considered (such as a new career or starting one's own business). As we will see, it is important to resist the temptation to see a sabbatical purely as a cost.

Faced with the sabbatical literature at hand, I drew one fundamental conclusion. I do not believe in "one-size-fits-all" solutions for sabbatical planning any more than financial planners would advocate this approach for financial or retirement planning. So I did my own research, distilled my own experiences as a project planner who has worked and lived abroad, and developed a framework that can help anyone plan their own *custom-built* sabbatical. In this book, I will share this framework and my own sabbatical experiences in the hopes of providing useful advice to anyone who yearns for a break, for change, and for renewal. It is an achievable dream once you know how to make it work.

As we will see, planning is your secret weapon in making a sabbatical work. Remember, we plan for major life events like marriage, having and raising children, taking care of elderly parents, and retirement. We open college tuition savings accounts, fund retirement and pension plans, and open elder-care accounts for these purposes. Before having children, we take Lamaze and first-aid classes, read up on how to raise a baby, buy cribs and other things, and so on. We realize our major values like charity via contributions, volunteer work, or funding charitable foundations. Business plans and start-up capital are the fuel that makes any new business work.

These life events are all significant, exciting, expensive, and if we are honest with ourselves a little bit scary! But we make them possible – indeed, successful – by planning for them. Taking a sabbatical is no different. What is different is that the bookstores are filled with titles giving financial-planning advice, business start-up guidance, retirement-planning assistance, and so on. There is a growing genre of self-help books that aims to assist people in better managing their time, and developing the right habits to become more successful. I hope one day we have the same depth of resources for planning a sabbatical – which in many ways is a particularly potent time-management tool and success builder alike.

What I will do in this book is talk about a "power sabbatical." I define a power sabbatical as a sabbatical focused not just on rest and rejuvenation, but also on achieving greater life and career focus and achievement. As the "power walk" has an aim beyond just getting from point A to point B, and the "power nap" is about more than just sleep, the power sabbatical serves many needs. It often involves some elements of a "working sabbatical" and usually involves some careful financial planning. A power sabbatical is most definitely not just a long and expensive vacation!

1.3 The roots

A world-changing idea for maintaining our physical, social, spiritual, and financial health was presented to us thousands of years ago, which we continue to ignore at our own peril. We have adopted so many of the Bible's precepts in our own lives and in our societies – but not so with sabbaticals, the Biblical principle of an extended period of rest. Because the Biblical context of a sabbatical was that of an agricultural society, we have most likely taken the Biblical instructions to "rest the land" a bit too literally, as we overlook how necessary this is especially in our post-industrial world.

With many other commandments, Biblical commentators have succeeded in applying the specific to the general. If your ox gores a neighbor's ox, you are liable to your neighbor for damages. This very agricultural example is the basis of Biblical laws of compensation for damages, which have been codified into the secular civil law of many nations. Indeed this law applies as much to causing damage to your neighbor's sport-utility vehicle (SUV) as to their ox! The sabbatical is another powerful concept that has meaning well beyond its agricultural roots.

But let's start at the roots of a sabbatical – the Sabbath. For all the religious traditions that take the Hebrew scriptures seriously, there is a familiar teaching called the Sabbath; this term originates from the Hebrew word *shabbath* meaning "to rest". But there is more than the Sabbath or "day of rest" that occurs every week on the seventh day. Every seventh year is known in the Bible as the Sabbatical year, and every 50th (seven times seven plus one) year is known as the Jubilee year.

The weekly Sabbath is observed by the religions based upon the Bible, each in its unique manner. All incorporate the concept of rest and dedication to spirituality. This weekly Sabbath is frequent but all-too-quickly over. When do we have the opportunity to immerse ourselves more fully in the world, to change our direction and to grow in meaningful ways that help ourselves and others around us? This is the purpose of the Sabbath year, the sabbatical. In the agricultural Hebrew society, it was a year that people would take off from work and dedicate themselves to God. In that year, wealth, land, possessions, and personal status did not matter. Debts were forgiven. Crops were neither planted nor harvested, and everyone learned that rich and poor are equal before God as even slaves were freed from work. The people are promised that if they trust in God, they will have a bumper crop in the sixth year, which will last them through the sabbatical year.

Contemplate and savor the sabbatical's meaning: trust in and reliance on God, communal social justice, freedom, relinquishing control, individual renewal, and return to the source. Indeed, giving up control over others and over the earth is a meaningful and restful experience. It is part of establishing a "rhythm" in life – work, rest/renew, work more effectively, rest/renew, and work ever more effectively. This rhythm is especially important if we want to move harmoniously through the typical life cycles (birth, schooling, working, marriage/partnership, having children, retiring, and so on).

Even outside the Biblically based religions, there are traditions that call for time to reflect, to release ourselves from our attachments, to be calm, to spend time with family and community, to refrain from doing, and to simply exist, love, and contribute. The ancient practices of the sabbatical provide tremendously effective ways of coping with the modern problems of overwork, stress, and change in our post-industrial economy. The idea of regular periods of rest is consistent with the natural order, after all. People need rest – we sleep an average of six to eight hours every day, and more when we are sick or very tired.

But a prolonged sabbatical rest period seems at first glance to be impractical even to those of great faith. How can an individual or family survive without a source of monetary sustenance for so long? Indeed, how could society sustain itself with the decreased productivity that would result – not to mention the loss of jobs key to the public good?

The Bible teaches us to have faith that we will be provided and cared for. Certainly faith and a support system are important, especially – as this book will explain – when reinforced with the proper mind-set and bolstered with good planning. In fact, we will see that the shift from an agricultural economy to today's knowledge economy, with the proliferation of new technologies, makes taking a sabbatical easier and even more necessary than in Biblical times.

However, the concept of the sabbatical had not spread far until the late nineteenth century, when Harvard University instituted sabbatical programs for their instructors; after which more American then European universities took up the practice. The purpose of the programs, typically lasting from six months to a year, was to provide an element of rest but even more so an opportunity for professors to advance in their craft by doing research and writing. Judging from how widespread the idea became (most universities offer such programs now), it must have reaped benefits. Later, we will see that the concept of the working sabbatical easily extends this idea to individuals outside of academia.

1.4 Selfish?

Isn't all this a bit selfish? We are trained to believe in the supremacy of work above nearly everything else – but this thinking is misguided. There is a strong undercurrent in society that makes us feel guilty if we do things for ourselves, particularly if that "thing" is taking a sabbatical. The Protestant work ethic – the moral basis of many Western societies – teaches not just the utility, but the moral supremacy, of hard work. There is nothing wrong and everything right with taking time off to heal, regenerate, and reenergize. Should the overstressed, under-satisfied person continue to suffer? In fact, to believe so runs against the grain of nature and, for those of us who believe in the Bible, the way of God. There is nothing selfish about avoiding harmful drugs or fattening foods, or about subjecting yourself to a strenuous exercise regime in order to stay in shape. There is nothing selfish about staying healthy – and nothing selfish about taking sabbaticals to help maintain your physical, emotional, and even career in tip-top shape. The Bible advises us to take care of ourselves and to guard our health.

To release yourself from these false and dangerous feelings of guilt, dig down and uncover any judgments you may be holding against yourself. Do you feel that you are not good enough or deserving of what you want? Or are you concerned that the transition you are about to make will hurt someone in your life and that you'll be responsible for their pain? Or you may feel that you're not smart enough, resourceful enough, bold enough, or just plain "enough" to make this change. Acknowledge these judgments then forgive yourself for holding these mistaken perceptions about who you really are and what you are capable of achieving. These guilty feelings are the preconceived notions of others; make your own ideas and forge your own path with moral confidence and clarity.

1.5 Reckless?

There is a common perception that you need to be a risk-taker in order to take a sabbatical. I suppose that's true – but don't you also need to be a risk-taker to get married or enter into a relationship, raise children, change jobs, move to a new home, and do many other things? You need to be a risk-taker to change your life – but you do not need to be a daredevil. You simply need to crave change, and a degree of autonomy to make this change happen for yourself. And you need to visualize yourself meeting your sabbatical goals; by doing this, you will be prepared to face the obstacles that inevitably come up.

As we start to look at planning a sabbatical, it will become apparent that many of these obstacles are actually in your own mind. Not knowing what might happen if you leave your job, home, circle of friends and family, and routine can be very frightening. Fear of the unknown – even more so than money worries, which can be managed – can stop you from realizing your best and brightest dreams if you let it. The trick is realizing that you cannot eliminate your fear – but you can manage it. Your sabbatical plan is your single most powerful weapon for managing fear of the unknown, since its purpose is to impose structure, a degree of certainty, and contingency plans into your thinking. And nearly every problem has a solution, if you train yourself to look for one. The very nature of a sabbatical means that it will be an exciting opportunity to get more accustomed to dealing with the unknown and other risks. If you leave yourself no choice but to be successful – you will amaze yourself with what you are capable of.

Fear of failure should not leave you mired in misery. Define what failure would look like for you. Imagine the worst possible thing that might happen. Could you live with it if it does happen? Can you change course before it happens or after it happens? You can, of course, if you stop obsessing over failure. Rather, think of a sabbatical – indeed any life change – in terms of actions, results, course corrections, and more actions. You hope for certain results, which you may achieve, exceed, or miss entirely. Learn from these results, become smarter and tougher, change course where needed, and move on. If you want to fear something, fear not achieving what you want because you were afraid to try; fear growing old and feeble before realizing your dreams. How able physically, mentally, and emotionally will you be when you are older to experience the sabbatical and grow from it? Is there is any real reason not to make the changes you need, and to go on sabbatical?

Remember – we are built not just for thinking and reflection but for decisive action, survival, and the ability to realize our wants and needs. We are made to meet challenges in ways we often forget. After all the self-reflection and planning, you do have the capacity to transition to action mode and make it happen. Focus on the goal, commit to reaching it, and let loose.

This sort of self-confidence and focused, problem-solving, risk-management orientation is as valued in the corporate or government world as it is in small business. The most successful executives, leaders, and business people are individuals who can live with and manage their fear.

1.6 How to use this book

Ideally, you will come across this book well before you actually plan on taking a sabbatical – perhaps even when beginning a career. (In fact, the planning principles herein work just as well for arranging a "gap year" between university and work as for planning an early or mid-career sabbatical.) You could then read straight through and begin methodically planning according to the steps laid out in the book. But we all know that life doesn't always work out so neatly. Many of you will instead come across this book much later on, when beset by job problems or severe stress. Some may even pick it up after being fired – facing the potential for lots of non-working time up ahead.

Don't worry. The mission of this book is to impart the inspiration, tools, and know-how that can make a sabbatical work for you. This book will show you how to take your own, real-life situation in hand and plan a sabbatical given that situation, your financial resources, your career state and outlook, your family situation, your level of comfort with risk, and a host of other factors. We avoid a checklist or standard approach in favor of teaching you how to plan for yourselves, and when to also seek outside counsel in the form of accountants, tax professionals, and others.

You will see how you can turn around a horrible experience like getting laid off into one of the most wonderful periods of your life. We will see that a properly planned sabbatical may even offer tax advantages. A power sabbatical will be less expensive and less risky than many imagine. And most of all – the act of taking a sabbatical will help you unlock long-dormant talents and abilities and truly build your character in ways the daily work grind can never do.

If you expect to be told what type of sabbatical to take, or which sabbatical options are worth exploring, you are likely to be disappointed. Can any book reach out to you, read your mind, and know your circumstances, capabilities, limitations, and dreams? Instead, I will help you to do this for yourself by asking the questions that will lead you to the right knowledge you need to begin looking at different sabbatical alternatives and to formulate a plan.

What you should also expect to find in these pages is encouragement and inspiration. A marriage, after all, is about more than the mechanics of applying for a marriage license and combining homes, and retirement about more than financial planning. There are deeply emotional aspects to these life-changing decisions that must be borne into mind if these are to be successful undertakings. So it goes with a sabbatical. One other piece of advice shines through whenever speaking with sabbatical-takers – you need a sense of humor. Leave your "regular" life and lifestyle behind, and realize that this sabbatical will entail different standards of living, different experiences and people, life from a whole new perspective, and quite a bit of patience. You will have to draw upon the ability to laugh at your situation and yourself.

And there is no shame in asking for additional support from your friends, relatives, or from a coach. In fact, enough of the right kind of help can make a seemingly difficult transition, relatively easy. Being a former lone-ranger, asking for and accepting help from others was difficult for me at first, but really made a difference once I got used to it. Now I wouldn't think of starting a major project or making a big change without relying heavily on my support system of close and loving friends, and my coach. Do whatever is necessary to make change easier.

In the end, knowledge is what you should aspire to. What I can guarantee is that you will know more about yourself and your ability to make a sabbatical happen and that you will have the tools to create a plan. The rest is up to you.

2: It's Time

2.1 Knowing

Many find it startling when they realize how clearly they know when the time has come for a sabbatical. There is a longing for more out of life. People search for greater fulfillment, want to accomplish what is important to them, and want to make healthier choices. Other times, the main driver for change is eliminating or controlling life's negative forces. Stress, a stalled career, overwork, overbearing managers, flagging creativity, and a disappearing personal life are prime examples. And the frenetic pace of change and presence of new threats in the world, in the workplace, and in our families can provide their own signposts towards a sabbatical.

Stress and job dissatisfaction alone are one of the most common and justified reasons for taking a sabbatical. According to the U.S. National Institute for Occupational Safety and Health (NIOSH), 40% of workers reported that their job was stressful, 25% view their jobs as the number one stress factor in their lives, with job stress and dissatisfaction accounting for the number one source of health complaints. A Gallup poll conducted in 2000 showed that up to 80% of workers feel stress on the job, nearly half say they need help in learning how to manage stress and 42% say their co-workers need such help. The U.K. Health and Safety Executive's 2004/5 research reported that one in six workers suffered from extreme stress. Recent research by the Samaritans, the U.K. emotional support charity, found that one third of Britons surveyed cited work as their biggest stress factor.

We don't have to dig too deeply to see what is causing this stress: people are working harder and losing their time off. A recent study by the Families and Work Institute reports that 33% of people are in contact with work at least once a week outside of normal working hours, and 37% take vacations shorter than seven days because of work demands. In other words, we don't even take advantage of the stingy time off we are given – according to a Harris Interactive survey taken in 2005, Americans gave away over 421 million vacation days!

Technological connectivity, increased transportation alternatives, fast package delivery services, and the proliferation of home offices are blurring the lines between work and free time. What makes it even worse is the culture of many organizations today expects its workers to sacrifice their vacation time on the altar of being "a company person," "a team player," and dedicated to their job. *"Of course you can take vacation, but...you'll have your BlackBerry smartphone with you, won't you?"* In this ultra-competitive world, it is easy to appear replaceable or dispensable if you take a vacation at the "wrong" time.

This phenomenon is worldwide. Even back in 1992, a United Nations Report labeled job stress "The 20th Century Disease" and a few years later the World Health Organization said it had become a "World-Wide Epidemic." A subsequent European Commission survey found that approximately half of the nearly 150 million workers in the European Union complained of job-stress factors like tight deadlines and boring work. And research from Finland published in *Psychosomatic Medicine* in 2006 found that among nearly 800 Finnish workers who were tracked for 28 years, those who said they often failed to "recover" from their work-week stress were more likely to eventually die of cardiovascular disease. In contrast, those surveyed who said they had usually recovered from their work stress were three times less likely to die of this cause.

2.2 Signs of overstress

How do you know if you are overstressed? Of course, a physical checkup and stress test can reveal the presence of stress, and should be a necessary starting point for anyone. Certain stress factors can be inherited, while others are acquired. There are personality, psychological, and situational factors that indicate overstress, and some personality tests you can do to uncover these factors. Ask yourself these questions:

- Are the boundaries between work and home blurry? Do you often take work home? Have you missed important family or social commitments?
- Are you a perfectionist?
- Are you a workaholic? Do others perceive you to be this way?
- Are you easily disappointed in people?
- Are you often exhausted, angry, or tense?

- Are you taking more and more sick and personal days just to escape work and the office? Is stress involved in this decision?
- Are you working harder and accomplishing less; in effect, running faster just to keep up on the treadmill of life?
- Does life seem too difficult to cope with at times?
- Do you experience guilt about being away from your family for work reasons, either for travel, or long hours?
- Do you feel excessively drained or fatigued?
- Do you ignore your health, or are you having health problems?
- Do you often find yourself angry or even infuriated at work?
- Do you seem to have no time for anyone?
- Do you tend to do things quickly, and are you constantly watching the clock? Do you get impatient when someone else slows you down?
- Do you tend to eat, drink, or smoke more when you are tense?
- Do you tend to "multi-task", even at home?
- Do you tire easily?
- Do you worry excessively about work or other parts of your life?
- Have you been forgetting routine tasks, appointments, birthdays, and other personal events?
- Have you been seeing family and friends less than usual?
- Have you made work-related errors lately, more so than usual? Have they been noticed?
- Have you stopped "growing" on the job? Are you no longer acquiring new skills? Is work no longer a challenge?
- Have you thought about being your own boss? Do you like the idea of having some control over your financial destiny? Do you crave structuring your own work?
- When describing your job to others, do you often use pessimistic or angry expressions?
- Would you admit to being burned out? Do others perceive you this way?

If you find yourself nodding your head more often than not to these questions, then it's likely you are facing significant amounts of stress. Particularly if you answered "yes" to the work-related questions, it is likely that work-related stress is a significant factor. Either way, take a note of those questions you answered "yes" to, since they will be used in your self-assessment and to help set the goals of your sabbatical.

There is no question that controlling stress is important, and that higher job satisfaction often leads to lower stress. But what surprises many is the extent of this relationship – people who enjoy what they do for a living actually live longer. A Duke University study showed that job satisfaction, more than any other single factor, was the biggest component of a longer life span! If you do not enjoy what you do for a living, a sabbatical can help you discover a new and better direction for yourself. And if you already like what you do, a sabbatical can return you to it with new vigor.

2.3 Invest in yourself

The media is replete with advice on how to invest your money. Stocks, bonds, retirement accounts, real estate – these are all worthy causes. But you are the worthiest cause. You do not stop investing early in your working career – for the investments to grow and pay off you need to keep investing. Likewise, your investment in yourself cannot stop when you get out of school. Continuing education, job training, spiritual development, and commitment to exercise and good health are great examples of ways to keep this momentum, and few would question their investment value. Permitting yourself time off to de-stress, think, and develop is, likewise, a worthy investment. Let's explore this further.

Financial planners tend to dislike the premise that you should take money (savings, investments) that you have today to use for a sabbatical now or in the future. Indeed, the "time value of money" means that $40,000 or so in your savings, pension, or other investments today could grow, through the compounding of interest or investment return rates, to hundreds of thousands of dollars in 20 or 25 years. So, they will argue, is your sabbatical worth all that?

There are three reasons I will answer "yes" to that question – two financial, and one wellness-related. First, don't think for a second that the $40,000 (or whatever it is) will be irrevocably lost in the first place. Taking a sabbatical – a power sabbatical – can lead to higher earnings and greater wealth after the sabbatical if you manage to get a better job, new higher-paying career, or start a business. And in a non-financial sense, just remember that no one can put a price on happiness. Happiness can compound over the years – and so can misery. Doctors agree that stress, depression, and malaise have very real and very damaging effects on your health. If you are overstressed or depressed, your medical costs may be much higher. And since your health is the ultimate constraint on your earnings power, think about the lost income if you cannot work properly. Finally, people are working longer and longer and retiring later; with one or more sabbaticals under your belt, you may be extra ready and able to do this when the time comes. Moreover, you will not be "waiting until retirement" to have new experiences and see the world – you'll be doing this on your sabbaticals! The longer you are able to work, the less money you need to target for retirement anyway. Factor these arguments into time value of money calculations!

2.4 Change – the only constant

Corporate life isn't what it used to be. With each passing year, the number of jobs an individual will hold over their working lifetime increases and the amount of time they remain in a single job decreases. The belief in loyalty between an employer and an employee has crumbled with social change, globalization, technological change, and increased competitive pressures. Jobs that have existed for years have now been automated and eliminated; at the same time, new types of jobs spring up all the time. Such "creative destruction" has occurred throughout history, but never at such a blinding pace, and never over such a sustained period of time. The Industrial Revolution was a painful time for those who worked with their hands, as they saw their jobs replaced by machines. Today's changes are no less challenging, but are occurring even faster.

Increased globalization, in the sense of freer flow of capital, people, knowledge, and technology, is one of the primary drivers of such change. Computer programmers, technicians, and technology architects were on top of the world in America in the 1990s. They were the gurus of the new machine, and received compensation, respect, and admiration. Yet after the turn of the century, things started going downhill for them. September 11th and the subsequent economic slowdown were matched by ever increasing amounts of foreign guest technology workers who would work at a fraction of the price of their American counterparts. At the same time, their American employers were increasingly outsourcing or off-shoring their jobs to cheaper locales.

It is a sad thing to witness these masters of the machine realizing that their prized skills and source of self-esteem are no more than a commodity, to be sold at the lowest price. Many have never recovered from this crash to their careers, egos, and finances, while others have adapted. Without analyzing the reasons that some thrive under adversity and others crumble, what I can say is that a sabbatical can teach us to see problems in terms of challenges and situations requiring solutions, rather than seeing them as threats or personal attacks, worthy only of complaints or excuses.

Whether you have a sabbatical or not you will still have to cope with change in your workplace. Though not everyone is equally affected by these changes, few are untouched. Your employer or clients are equally influenced by these changes, but our focus is on how changes impact you. Ask yourself these questions:

- Have these changes impacted you and your family already? How – emotionally, financially, socially, in other ways?
- How have recent developments in your industry affected your day-to-day job, and your longer-term career prospects?
- Have they already altered your income or prospects?
- Have you recently been unemployed?
- How do you expect that these changes will affect you in the next three to five years? What about further down the line?
- Do you see these changes as opportunities or threats?
- How prepared do you feel to meet these changes? What do you think you need to change about yourself to be better prepared?
- Do you find yourself constantly worrying about these changes?
- Do you feel that if you do not make some major changes to your career and/or your life, you may suffer a greatly reduced standard of living?

2.5 The "forced sabbatical"

Or maybe you are now confronting a "forced sabbatical." I'm a past member of that club myself. You were feeling secure in your full-time employment but that suddenly came to a screeching halt as you were "let go." What do you do now?

The first advice I have is not to panic. When the capacity to exert control over one's work, and over others, is suddenly taken away, it can lead to the collapse of the fired worker's self-esteem, professional status, and even standing within his or her own family. Yet as sharks smell blood, potential employers sense panic. Some will capitalize on the lack of self-esteem that comes from being fired, and offer you less than you are worth. Others will want to avoid you entirely.

You can try jumping right back into the fray and look for another job – or you can look at this as an opportunity to contemplate what lies ahead. I did the former and quickly found another job – after all, being unemployed with a family to support seemed inconceivable. It was only when that job was not working out that I realized that I was part of the problem. I began really considering what I wanted. I longed for a break, but I also wanted to begin writing and to be my own boss. The seeds of my sabbatical were sown.

Say to yourself: "I have all this time now – what do I want to use it for?" Why not take a sabbatical, refresh yourself, retrain, and come back to the working world stronger, smarter, and armed with new skills – if not entirely new goals? Why not grant your life the balance it so craves, so that your entire self-worth, identity, and dignity as a human being is not tied into one at-risk job or another, but to who you are, what you mean to your loved ones, and what you contribute to your community. You can also use a sabbatical to take back your career, and become independent (as a consultant, freelancer, or business owner).

But it depends upon you. Which path to take when a sabbatical is a forced one depends upon a number of things such as your marketability, your financial situation (including any severance payments you might have received), and your family situation. I will show you how to assess your situation and make an informed decision. Many of the planning techniques that I teach (such as saving and investing money for your sabbatical) will need to be "compressed" or eliminated in your case, but I will show you how to do this.

2.6 The "mid-life" crisis

Are you undergoing a mid-life crisis? Wait a minute now – when is "mid-life"? The fact is that a mid-life crisis can happen in one's thirties, forties, fifties – whatever. This is probably not a great term to use, but we all understand what it means so I will use it here: at some point, you become tired or disillusioned and begin to question.

You ask yourself about what you really want to do – are you getting satisfaction from your work, your financial condition, your home and home life? You may wonder what happened to your childhood dreams, your core needs, your sense of "purpose." Is there enough time in your life for your religious or social community, for yourself, for your hobbies, and for the things you want to do? And if you feel stifled by work, family, or other obligations and constantly fantasize about being somewhere else you know something needs to change

The trouble is that the day-to-day of living and surviving often overtakes us, and does not allow us the time, solitude, and quiet to reflect on and answer these difficult questions. A sabbatical can be a perfect opportunity to do this – and to reposition your life the way you want it to be.

2.7 Creativity lost

Let's now turn inward some more. Do you find that your creativity is depleted? Nearly any job nowadays requires some degree of creative thinking. But creativity is your bread and butter if you are in a "creative" field (the arts, writing), research, academic, product or software development, or any other endeavor that requires you to develop new ideas or design new ways of doing things. If your creativity is flagging, your job performance will suffer greatly.

There is no cut and dried solution to this problem, but many in the creative fields agree that rest, a change of pace, and a change of location can awaken the creative muse. While a sabbatical can be taken anywhere (even in your own home), a power sabbatical – to the extent that it involves growth and creative development – will often entail entirely new surroundings.

2.8 Our time here is short

Keep looking inward, even as we contemplate the outside world. The tragedies of September 11th have taught everyone a very simple lesson. Life is short. It can, tragically, be very short. So we must make the most of it – we never know which day will be our last, even if we are young, healthy, and sitting behind a desk working. Keeping this in mind, do we really want to be stuck in a job we hate or put off our dreams and goals?

Here I use September 11th as an example of any extreme life-changing event that can affect you – whether others are also affected or not. Perhaps you have just experienced a more personal life-altering event – good or bad. The sudden death of a loved one, a large unexpected inheritance, the destruction of your home in a hurricane, the discovery that you have serious health problems, or that you have just defeated them – all of these will change your life in ways you cannot even comprehend right now.

Remember this simple truth as you read through this book, contemplate your own sabbatical, plan for it, and do it. At any point in the process you may stop and turn back, out of fear of the unknown. Maybe you long to go abroad but are afraid of terrorism at your destination. Or maybe you are afraid to give up a steady income stream. Or you might have made your move and started a sabbatical – only to return to your life when the first challenge reared its head. You need to know that even if you reject a sabbatical because of this fear, there is no guarantee that things will be OK if you remain where you are in your life. Terrorism, crime, or health problems can happen anyway, and seemingly safe jobs can disappear in a heartbeat.

I know this from my own experience. I've lived through all of the embarrassing examples above, before developing the mind-set and planning approach that I'm now sharing with you. What caused me to change my thinking was my last failed attempt at a sabbatical in a part of the world that always fascinated me – the Middle East. I returned to my native New York after finally arranging and beginning a working sabbatical in Israel which would have involved travel throughout the region and Mediterranean; I was concerned about political violence. So my wife, daughter, and I returned to New York City. I thought about that decision much over the years, but never so much as on a bright sunny September day just a few months later, when the Middle Eastern political violence we were running from came to find us. Fortunately none of us were in the Twin Towers that day, but we were close enough to see the fires burning and smell that awful smoke as we fled the city on foot. Even then, the irony of our choice to cut short our sabbatical cut through the smoke and fire.

2.9 Moderation

Let's stay with the symbolism of September 11th. It is not going out on a limb to say that the events of that day represented a clash of values, and the presence of extremism. And it is no secret that extreme conditions beget extreme ways of thinking and living. Whether economic deprivation (or extreme wealth), rigid social homogeneity, extreme beliefs, or a host of other extremes – the effects on a society and a person can be deleterious. Look at the extremes in your life. You might be one of those people with the dubious honor of having an "extreme commute" to work. You might work very long hours regularly or travel for work nearly all the time.

What has this done to your ways of thinking – do you tend to think, speak, or act in extreme terms? Perhaps a sabbatical can help you seek the moderation, balance, and harmony that we all need in our lives.

There is a reason that many great ethical thinkers suggest moderation as a better path than extremism. Life according to any one or more extremes becomes formulaic, robotic – obeying a strict set of rules and no more. This denies our very essence as humans and not animals – the ability to choose, think for ourselves, and the ability to exercise free will. That is the very essence of humanity. By allowing you to rest, and regain control of your life by giving up the reins for a little while, a sabbatical salves the extremist trends in all of our lives.

2.10 What a sabbatical can do for you

2.10.1 SELF-CONFIDENCE

Some of us have tremendous reserves of self-confidence; others feel that they lack self-esteem and courage. Remember the characters in The Wizard of Oz – the lion thought he lacked courage, but had plenty, as did the Tin Man with a heart, and the Scarecrow with a brain. The Wizard of Oz simply provided "validation," and the rest was easy.

I will play the Wizard for just a moment: think about what you have already achieved in life. You may have a long-lasting link to a life partner, possibly even managed to raise a child (or children). You may have completed college, or vocational training, or more, or achieved success in a career. Do you think planning and taking a successful sabbatical can be that hard compared to what you have achieved already? Maybe your achievements lie in sports or games. No one needs to tell you how much hard work goes into training for athletic success – or success on the chessboard, for that matter. You can apply that same dedication and spirit to planning a sabbatical, with the simple tools we have been discussing. Perhaps your field is the performing or creative arts. Then practice, craftsmanship, and creativity are the tools of your trade – and these are the very same qualities that will serve you well when crafting a sabbatical plan.

If you are feeling that you are not so good at anything, take heart and stop comparing yourself to others (admit it, that's what you are doing). Doing so is self-defeating. Achievement and success are relative to your own capabilities. We find out fairly early in life that we are not all endowed with the same capabilities, or the same resources. The only way you can measure success is relative to your own individual (and realistic) goals. If you are starting out in the real-estate development field, it might be quite an achievement to finance and construct your own apartment building. But you cannot expect your first-year sales and profit margins to approach those of Donald Trump.

Set your own goals, and rejoice in your progress towards achieving them. The sabbatical will help you build up and fortify your self-confidence, and this will have a ripple effect throughout your life. It will also foster a greater sense of responsibility, as you take the reins of your life and start to make positive changes via your sabbatical.

2.10.2 TIME FOR YOURSELF

You need time off to recover – or time off to be joyful. You need time to do what you want to do, and time to do what you need to do for yourself. You need time to plan your life and career and get it on the track you want it on – which means you need time to think. You may also need time to actually make the changes you've planned. And even aside from these very practical goals – you may want time for your own wants and desires, to rediscover old hobbies or develop new ones, to stimulate creativity, and to free your mind. In other words, you want to bring balance back into your life – balance between work and play, balance between family, friends, and self.

This means more than just an hour or so at the end of a tiring day, or a bit of time on a weekend (after you've caught up with your chores, social activities, and family activities). It even means more than the two or three week vacation which many of us get each year; this vacation can be a slice of heaven, but when one considers the time and effort preparing for some vacations and the time and effort "recovering" from one – at work and at home – the effect is short-lived at best. Does anyone really believe a two-week vacation can relieve accumulated stress from an unpleasant and unsatisfying workplace plus home pressures? Consider how much more relief would you get from a year off.

2.10.3 BRING ABOUT CHANGE

Think about this: many have their teenage years to consider what they may want to do in life, and to prepare for university or vocational training. They then may have a few to several more years of this education or training ahead of them after that; during this time they may gain confidence in their decision, or change their minds and study plans entirely. But then – bang. That's it. Start a job or a career, and work till retirement. How many eighteen or twenty-one year olds really know for sure what they will do for the rest of their working lives? Even if they do – what happens when changes in the global economy lay waste to their best-laid plans and eliminate the jobs they envisioned? We need one or more lengthy breaks along the way to take stock, challenge our assumptions and life path, and recalibrate – or retool entirely.

This is not to say that people cannot make major changes to their lives and careers without a sabbatical. But how many more of us, not as practiced in the art of extreme multi-tasking, would have, had we only the time to think.

This is also not to say that the changes need be major – just significant. You may need to bring your skills up to keep ahead in the workplace or in your business, but your travel or work schedule does not allow you to take evening classes. Time off from work may be your best option here.

A sabbatical can also help you if you're hitting a glass ceiling at. It can do this by giving you time to: develop your creativity; hone your skills; look for another job; try an entirely new career; or start your own business or freelancing career.

2.10.4 JOIN THE GLOBAL VILLAGE

It is a bit trite to say, but nonetheless true that we are now members of a global village. Some however are more comfortable and successful in this village than others, and it should not be difficult to forecast which of these will achieve greater financial success in the long run. Experience gained living and working abroad can help develop a more flexible outlook and sensitivity to other views, backgrounds, and cultures. Barriers between cultures, religions, and economic backgrounds can be broken down.

With a sabbatical, you will become more reliant on your own experiences and judgment, and less "programmed" to regurgitate those of your primary culture and environment. You will also begin to understand, if not accept or even embrace, other cultures, races, classes, and ways of doing things. That is what it really means to be "worldly."

A sabbatical can also train you to think and act more creatively, and the experiences you take in during a sabbatical can enhance your own originality and creativity. This is important whether or not you are involved in a "creative" field, since in today's work world a creative approach is a competitive edge in nearly any type of job.

2.11 What a sabbatical cannot do

A sabbatical must come at the right time in one's life, for a poorly-timed or a poorly-planned sabbatical can just make life even worse. Another qualification needs to be made. It is also important to recognize when you have other problems that need addressing, problems that a sabbatical cannot solve. A sabbatical should not be used as a way of running away from problems that should be met head-on.

A sabbatical can provide rest, relaxation, physical activity, or a change of climate and this can alleviate some problems. However, if your symptoms are causing you serious physical, emotional, or mental health problems, you should see a doctor to be sure. Your symptoms may have medical and psychosomatic causes or they may be symptoms of job stress and dissatisfaction. If problems at work are due to untreated attention deficit disorder, general restlessness, or dyslexia, a sabbatical alone – without the necessary medical support – may not be your answer. In some cases, marital or other family problems or family care issues are another; however, togetherness during a shared sabbatical experience can be just what the doctor ordered.

Further, and at the risk of stating the obvious, a sabbatical is not correctly timed if you don't have most of your core physical needs (sufficient health, money, sustenance, shelter, a safe living environment, and so on). Think of a sabbatical lying at a level above one's basic needs, where those basic needs must be met first.

One of your goals might be to meet that special someone. Perhaps you've undergone a divorce, or perhaps you have been trying without success to meet your match for quite a while. Sometimes the best thing can be a change of place and a change of circumstances to trigger that event. But it is important that this not be the sole goal of your sabbatical, or you may be disappointed. To avoid this (and at the same time to maximize your chances of meeting someone), you should carefully plan your sabbatical such that you may come into contact with other single, kindred spirits. Volunteer work in a cause you believe in, or targeting working and living in a religious, social, or cultural community that has personal meaning to you is a good way to do this. In such a situation, you will instantly have many things in common with those around you, and you should walk away from that experience with friends, or maybe more.

The key to understanding whether you need a sabbatical or just to stay and address your problems/issues is to ask yourself – and those close to you – what a sabbatical will do to address your problems. If the answer is simply "avoiding them," then you should reconsider your sabbatical plans. If you are in doubt, consider getting a professional opinion. For financial problems, discuss with a reputable financial planner; for health problems, with a physician/psychologist/ psychiatrist, and so on. Specific job challenges may best be addressed via a job or career change; or, if you are generally satisfied with your work but seek a better work-life balance, this can be achieved via measures like flex-time, compressed or reduced workweeks, job rotation, or remote working arrangements. Saying that, approaching a current or future employer about a job change is not always easy. Often these organizations may perceive (rightly or wrongly) that you do not have the skills or background needed to make such a change; in cases like these, a working sabbatical in your preferred field will be of enormous help. Also, you may not find it possible to make alternative working arrangements that permit you to be more involved with other aspects of your life. Here again, the sabbatical can allow you the time to make such connections.

3: Sizing Things Up

3.1 Personality assessment

It is tempting to put the cart before the horse and start planning your sabbatical now. But before looking outwards to a sabbatical, peer inwards. Take stock of your self and your situation. This will allow you to plan for the right sabbatical, and to pick the right time to take it.

Begin by asking who you are, what you feel your purpose is in the world, and what your moral, religious, ethical, and humanist values are. Write a biography of no longer than a paragraph (much as writers or speakers do in their writings or in promotional materials – but make sure to focus on the "whole person"). Look at this description again – have you described a job rather than a person? Does your description resound with a spoken or unspoken "but"? I am, or do, this, but I'd always wanted to be, or do, that. Leave those "buts" in there – they are key to your sabbatical goals as we will see. Then write a second paragraph. Talk about your talents, gifts, what is important to you, and what you enjoy, regardless of whether these applied to you in the past or now. Discuss how successful you feel in life and career.

Now put down some basic facts about yourself:

- Are you a giving person – do you enjoy helping or mentoring?
- Are you creative, imaginative, curious, a craftsperson, methodical, analytical, a problem-solver, a life-long learner?
- Are you satisfied with the responsibility and role that you have in life and/or work, status and reputation, and level of self-esteem?
- Do you get along well with new people and situations?
- How do you deal with risk, uncertainty, or lack of structure?
- How have you dealt with failure in your life?
- How well can you focus on your goals, or new projects?
- What do you see as your weaknesses?
- Why would you not take a sabbatical?

One may wonder where this is leading. Maybe certain personality types are more suited to sabbaticals than others. That is an interesting topic for further research. The way I like to view this question is whether certain personality types are more suited to certain types of sabbaticals; I believe this to be the case. Practically, this means matching your personality with the right sabbatical alternative – once you have defined your goals. If you are less comfortable with risk and unstructured environments, a highly structured, pre-planned sabbatical with a defined program structure and logistics might be the best options. If your definitions of success are to some extent set by your family, culture, or environment, then you may want to look into a sabbatical program that is consistent with this definition. On the other hand, if you are a freethinker who is comfortable with risk and uncertainty, you are likely to want a bit less definition around your sabbatical alternative (i.e., "this is roughly how I'd like to start, and we'll see how it goes from there"). Those who are extremely self-directed will want less "supervision" over their sabbatical than those who require external focus and guidance, the latter being better suited to packaged sabbatical programs, education, or volunteer opportunities. And those that are more comfortable with other people and social situations may desire a group setting for their sabbaticals, while individualists may go it on their own.

But let your self-assessment guide you in *how* to meet your goals – not in determining *what* those goals are. You may be an analytical person working as an engineer, but with an "inner guitarist" yearning to break through. The main purpose of the self-assessment is finding the best way to meet these goals. If the "inner guitarist" lives inside a person comfortable with risk-taking and unstructured environments, then semi-structured travel through Spain coupled with flamenco guitar lessons along the way may be one path to consider. If on the other hand more structure is needed or if you tend to be shy by nature, a pre-planned guitar camp may be a better answer.

It is also important to realize that a sabbatical is not just for people who "have it all together," and are focusing solely on self-improvement. A sabbatical can directly relate to your ability to be healthy (stress reduction, exercise, a new physical environment), to earn a better living (skills acquisition, situational awareness, cultural flexibility, starting a business, exploring and planning a career change, etc.), and to improve your social relationships and even a marriage (more time to spend with others, fewer distractions). On one hand, it is hard to plan and execute a sabbatical when dealing with basic issues of existence (food, clothing, shelter, health) – but, in fact, a well-timed sabbatical can actually affect these basic issues in the future.

3.2 Financial self-assessment

The aim of the financial self-assessment is to understand the components of your net worth, and your flow of income and expenses. Maybe you've already gone through this exercise on your own or with a financial planner; either way, it's not too hard to do. To prepare for this step, gather your bank and investment statements, credit card bills, and other financial records. Then fill in this spreadsheet, (see Table 3.1 Financial Records).

TABLE 3.1 FINANCIAL RECORDS

Assets	Value
Investments	
Annuities	
Bonds	
Cash value of insurance	
Education savings plans	
Pension	
Retirement accounts	
Stock options	
Stocks	
Trust fund	
Savings	
Cash	
Certificates of deposit	
Checking/savings/money market accounts	
Fixed assets	
Boats	
Cars	
Collections	
Electronics	
Equipment and tools	
Farm	
Furniture	
Home (first, second)	

Assets	Value
Other land/property	
Valuables (jewelry, furs, etc.)	
Car or boat loan	
Credit cards	
Home equity loan	
Installment loan	
Loan from pension plan	
Other loans, guarantees, posted collateral	
Mortgage	
Student loan	
Taxes due	

Income	Value
Alimony income	
Business income	
Capital gains	
Child-care income	
Commissions	
Financial windfall (insurance settlement, work-related settlement, inheritance, winning the lottery or other game, etc.)	
Grant income	
Investment income	
Limited partnerships/ownership in business ventures	
Pension income	
Portfolio income (dividends, income, capital gains, royalties)	
Rental income	
Salaries	
Sale of investments	
Sale of property/goods	
Savings/investment interest income	
Scholarship income	
Social security or other public assistance	
Tips	
Wages	

Outlays	Value
Education	
Adult education or classes	
Children's education/tuition	
School books/supplies	
Transport	
Airfare	
Car insurance	
Car payment	
Commuting (train/bus/metro fare, etc.)	
Gasoline	
Parking	
Financial payments	
Alimony payments	
Child-support payments	
Credit card payments	
Life insurance premium	
Loan fees and payments	
Long-term care insurance premium	
Other installment loan or line of credit repayment	
Other insurance premium	
Student loan payments	
Taxes (income, property, business, wealth)	
Entertainment	
Arts performances/concerts	
Cable TV	
Children's activities/camp	
Collections	
DVDs	
Gambling	
Health, golf, tennis club membership	
Hobbies	
Music	
Movies	
Other entertainment	
Sporting events	
Vacations/travel	

Outlays	Value
Miscellaneous	
Attorney and accountant fees	
Cash outlays	
Charitable contributions	
Gifts to others	
Jewelry/watches	
Other discretionary expenses	
Personal enrichment classes	
Pet care	
Professional dues	
Recreational "toys"	
Repairs	
Service contracts	
Shipping	
Storage costs	
Supplies	
Tools/instruments	
Health/Beauty	
Basic grooming	
Clothing/shoes	
Dental insurance	
Disability insurance premium	
Eye care and eyeglasses, contact lenses	
Haircuts	
Health insurance premium	
Laundry/dry cleaning	
Makeup/Manicures	
Massages	
Non-covered medical and dental expenses	
Non-covered prescription drugs	
Therapy	
Other child-care expenses	
Child / elder Care	
Child care	
Elder care	

Outlays	Value
Business expenses	
Business rent, utilities, communications, postage, equipment rental/leases, stationery, company vehicle, supplies, business insurance/ worker's compensation, employee's salaries, business taxes, advertising/promotions, business travel and entertainment, licensing costs, other service expenses	
Investments	
Financial advisor fees	
Funding savings/investment	
Investment loan repayment	
Meals	
Groceries	
Restaurants/bars	
Take-away/prepared meals	
Housing	
Alarm fees	
Home decoration	
Home maintenance	
Home remodeling	
Homeowner's/renter's insurance	
Lawn care	
Maintenance	
Mortgage/rental payment	
Snow removal	
Utilities	
Communications	
Internet service	
Landline and cell phones	

These categories may or may not all apply to you – but they should give you enough information to define the exact categories that do. You can now use this information to create your net worth statement (assets less liabilities) and net monthly income statement (monthly income less outlays). This information will be used to help you find sources of funds for your sabbatical. Basically, you can fund your sabbatical from using some of your net worth, taking on liabilities, or growing your net worth by increasing income, receiving grants, or reducing expenses.

A higher net worth or higher net income means more alternatives to choose from. But it is important to run through this exercise even if you feel you are living "hand to mouth." In some cases, you may be able to uncover sources of sabbatical money from your balance sheet or cash flow; if not, you may be able to borrow money, apply for scholarships or other funding, ask for gifts, or choose a low-cost sabbatical alternative like a stay-at-home sabbatical or a working sabbatical.

In the end, you are most likely going to be paying for your sabbatical from more than one source. If your sabbatical costs $70,000, you may get $5,000 from gifts, $25,000 from a home equity loan, $10,000 from the sale of stock, and $10,000 from working overtime or a second job before your sabbatical, and $20,000 from other sources during your sabbatical. As long as the numbers add up, you are on your way.

3.3 Sabbatical goals – a first try

With this awareness, it's time to start thinking at a high level about sabbatical goals. Do not yet worry about listing too many goals or setting what seem to be impractical goals – we will assess their feasibility and prioritize them later on. Instead, consider the following guidelines when making a list of goals:

- Are you looking to use a sabbatical to test drive a new career or start a business? Are you looking to return to the same job or type of work you currently do?
- Do you have weaknesses you would like to work on during your sabbatical?
- Do you want a sabbatical for you alone, or for your whole family? How can your family's various goals be met during your sabbatical? What are you willing to sacrifice in terms of your own goals in order to meet some of theirs?
- Do you want to "give back"? How can you use a volunteer opportunity to satisfy volunteering needs, or even to volunteer at an organization that might represent a career change or new job?

- Do you want to start or finish a personal project during a sabbatical? Are there other personal goals you wish to achieve?
- How would you like your life to have more meaning? What kind of practical steps would you take on sabbatical to start making this happen?
- Ideally, how would you describe your sabbatical to others after it is over?
- If you had a year to take off, all expenses paid, where would you go?
- If you keep a journal or blog, what do you find yourself writing about?
- If you were told you only had one year to live, what would you do?
- Think about the "buts" in your self-assessment, and think about your core values and talents. Are there any gaps between what you want to be and what you are?
- What about your life makes you miserable?
- What about your life would you change if you could? How would you reprioritize?
- What causes you to pause and reflect when reading, watching a movie, or speaking to people? What causes you to picture yourself differently?
- What changes would you make to be in greater harmony with your self and your values? What kind of steps would this entail?
- What is your obsession?
- What kind of practical experiences, programs, work, training, or education would you engage in to start filling those gaps?
- What thoughts and feelings pop into your mind when meditating or reflecting that you would love to act on?

3.4 Types of sabbaticals

All sabbaticals should also include elements of rest and rejuvenation. But a Power Sabbatical is also oriented towards *exploring, learning,* or *growing.* Think about how you would categorize the goals you are defining. For example, if you are hoping to reconnect with your family or spiritual, religious, ethnic, or social communities, or if you are trying to improve some of your weaknesses (shyness, public-speaking problems, excessive risk aversion, etc.) this would normally be a *growing* goal. Learning a new discipline or advancing in your current field (getting a graduate degree, doing post-graduate work, and so on) would be a *learning* sabbatical, as would be developing new technical skills. An *exploring* sabbatical may at first seem less directed (actually, it is!). The idea is to try out something new – a new career, job, business, hobby, sport, spiritual practice, living location and standard, and so on. You may or may not be prepared to commit to follow through with this new something – just to try it. It is important to classify your sabbatical goals to better understand and define these goals.

We've just classified sabbaticals based on the "why." Another way to do this is based on where. A sabbatical can take place in your home, elsewhere nearby, somewhere else in your country, or out of the country entirely. It can take place in one fixed location, by traveling constantly, or anything in between. And then there is the "how," as in, how you will finance your sabbatical. You can do this by saving for it, selling assets, borrowing money, obtaining gifts or grants, working while on sabbatical, or any combination of these.

Don't be afraid if your sabbatical goals are not overly precise yet – you want to think "big picture" now. Also do not rule out certain goals because you don't think they are realistic. Once you start more detailed research of sabbatical alternatives and start planning, you will then assess feasibility, which may require adjusting or changing goals.

So at this stage, your high level goals might resemble the following:

"I want to learn more about my wife's native Chile. I would like to spend time with her family there, learn the language, and tour around."

"I want to try something new work-wise – maybe buy a franchise or start a business – but I'm not sure what kind yet."

"I want to finally finish my masters degree in Asian studies – and I'd love to do that work in Asia."

"I seem to miss out on promotions at work because I don't have the interpersonal skills they seem to want in a higher manager. I want to learn to play golf, improve my public speaking, and gain confidence in social situations."

These examples of goals are not yet plans – but they point us in the right direction to do our research.

3.5 Write it down

At this juncture, make sure you've written down what we've just discussed:

- Self description
- Talents, gifts, and personality assessment
- Situational assessment
- Financial assessment
- What you love – and what you hate
- Initial goals

4: Goal Setting

4.1 The next stage of goal-setting

We've already started the process of goal discovery at a very high level. You have a better awareness as to who you are, what you want, and your own definition of success. You have expressed a high-level vision for what you want to get from your sabbatical, desired experiences, learning opportunities, and how you want to be changed. Now it's time to dig a bit deeper, and clearly define the sabbatical goals.

When thinking about goals, remember that a goal can only be achievable if it is specific, feasible, and can be measured somehow. A specific goal will address in detail what you want to accomplish, how you want to do it, where you intend to do it, when you plan on doing it, and why. A feasible goal is something that, given your personal, financial, and physical capacities, you can reasonably attain. Quite simply, a goal is measurable if you know you have reached it. Let's look at some examples to understand this better.

Say you have initially defined one of your sabbatical goals as to "advance academically to further your career." This goal may be feasible for you (providing you can afford and be accepted into an academic program) but is not specific and is not measurable. Let's work on it. A more specific goal may be to "enroll in a one-year (when) graduate certificate program in Web-services development (what and how) at New York University (where) that would qualify you for promotion to project manager at your organization (why)." It is pretty easy to measure success with this goal – passing the course and obtaining the certificate!

4.2 Goal mapping

As you begin to define your goals, you stand in a middle ground between the dreams, self-knowledge, and the mundane specifics of an actual plan. You will now define your base assumptions about the sabbatical – how long you think you will take off, how much you estimate your sabbatical might cost, how you think you will finance your sabbatical, how much time you think you need to plan and prepare for your sabbatical, and other aspects of the sabbatical that bear special consideration. You should also define risks to your sabbatical's success (such as not being able to find the right work while on sabbatical, underestimating the amount of money required for the sabbatical, not being able to find work immediately after returning from sabbatical, and so on). How to do this is best demonstrated via examples.

Map out on paper all of your personal goals. If you are finding that your goals are many, try to aggregate them into more general categories (e.g., "spending more time with family" instead of "attending daughter's concerts," "helping son with homework," and "visiting parents more often.") Draw these as circles, with the name of the goal inside. Then try to map out your professional/career goals in the same manner. Where do these overlap? The overlaps are the areas you need to think about seriously as your sabbatical goals – providing you can afford to see these goals through, which we will address when talking about feasibility. The best way to see this approach is through examples (see Figure 4.2 My Goal Mapping).

Figure 4.2 My Goal Mapping

Career goals   Personal goals

Spend more time writing

Learn more about my background and religion

Expose our daughter to other languages and cultures

Live in Israel with family for a while

Build my consulting business

Take a break from long days and harsh weather

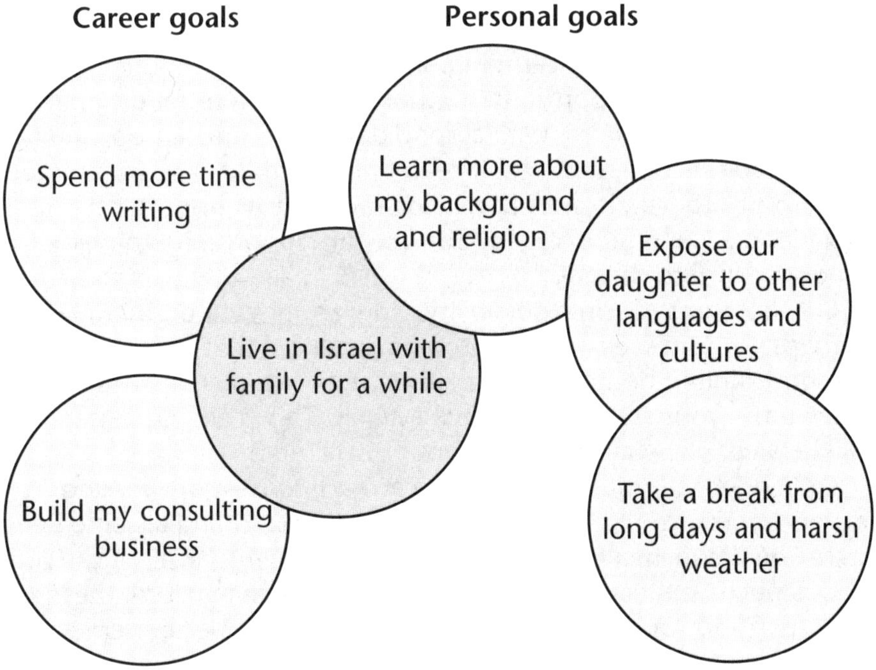

This is a mapping of my own sabbatical goals. Career goals are at the left, while personal goals are at the right. The intersection of these goals, a period of time living in Israel, allowed me to satisfy my personal goals as well as some specific professional goals (having more time to write, and coming up with a more specific consultancy business plan, a web site, and so on). Let's look at some more examples to understand this mapping process even better.

Let's say you are a commercial photographer, working on contract for two or three sports publications. You would like to open your own photography studio, and split your time freelancing and teaching. But to do so, you need to build up a more diverse portfolio of works (beyond sports photography) and make contacts you can leverage as a freelancer. Those are career goals. Now let's look at your personal goals. Your life as a contract photographer is quite stressful; one of the most stressful elements is the need to be at a sporting event at a moment's notice, and another is the need to travel all around the country to these events constantly. One personal goal is to reduce your level of stress and stay in one place for a while. But another is to spend more time in the outdoors, exercising and taking better care of your health.

Where is the overlap? Thinking about this, one interesting possibility for a sabbatical might be to stop working on these contracts for a year and plan several excursions into the great outdoors. These can be within reasonable distance of where you live, and can include rafting/boating, hiking, camping, and so on. Such experiences also offer an excellent opportunity to photograph nature, birds, animals, people, and much more. With a good digital camera, laptop, and fast Internet connection, these could lead to the birth of a freelance career if these photographs are offered for sale. But as importantly, such experiences will offer excellent exercise, an opportunity to enjoy the outdoors, and to de-stress.

But that's not the only possibility. How about your desire to teach? Perhaps you can seek out a photography school that will take you on for some limited hours – either paid or as a volunteer. If you still have extra time, you can do the above as well. This teaching experience will be valuable when you open your own studio.

Let's now say you are a health-care administrator working in a major city. You would like to move up in your clinic, and at some point start your own health-care clinic. As with many large cities, your population is multicultural. Therefore, experience in one of these key cultures (and language skills) can help you to better serve your clientele. A sabbatical abroad in one of these cultures sounds like the obvious choice. But if this sabbatical also involves working or volunteering in a health-care capacity – get ready for a career breakthrough!

Here is another scenario. You are a senior-level accountant, trying unsuccessfully for years to become a chief financial officer or finance director. Your technical accounting expertise is top par, but something is stopping you from being promoted to that top slot. First, you need to find out what it is. Ask senior management which trait, characteristic, skill, or set of experiences would propel you to that role if you had it. Also see what you can figure out based on the backgrounds of the current and past holders of that position. If they were all friends of the Chief Executive Officer (CEO) and you are not, then the organization you are working for may be wrong for you. Possibly they all have expertise outside of accounting: one was a country manager of an Asian subsidiary, another worked in sales. Perhaps at your organization experience working in another country is a de facto requirement for that position. This knowledge lets you home in on a career goal: gaining international work experience and/or gaining experience outside of accounting, so that you will be "promote-able."

Now let's focus on personal goals. Your wife, originally from Argentina, would like to spend more time there to be with family and to introduce your children to her native land and culture. You see this as a great adventure possibility, and an excellent opportunity to become closer to her and to your kids.

What types of sabbatical opportunities would take advantage of the overlap of career and personal goals? You have several possible paths. First, you could find similar work to your current job at an Argentine concern (which gives you the international experience). Or perhaps your wife's family owns a medium-sized meat-processing plant. They might be able to arrange for you to work (perhaps on a part-time contract basis) in the finance office alongside the finance manager, or in a front-line function like sales, marketing, or such. That would give them the benefit of your home-country experience and language skills (not to mention your background as an accomplished accountant) and you the benefit of international experience in another type of industry sector, and possibly doing another type of job.

What if you do a job search there and no one appears to be willing to offer anything other than full-time work? You then have a couple of alternatives. First, you can agree to work full time, at least for part of your sabbatical. Next, you can "educate" them as to various less than full-time ways that enable you to enjoy and benefit from your new environment, and them to benefit from your skills and experience. Perhaps they will agree to have you work five or six hours a day, providing it is during part of the working day of your home country (if they do business with them). This may involve working on the early, or on the late, side of the day. But they may see strong benefits here and may agree to less than a full-time schedule. Or you could offer a "compressed workweek" – say three days of ten hours each (which adds up to nearly a full-time week). Alternatively, you would work out other arrangements whereby you agree to work a certain number of hours or days per month, which is less than a full-time schedule – but you let your new employer set the days you will work.

To start my sabbatical, I managed to convince the customer I was contracting for to keep me on for only a couple of weeks per month, for the first four months of the sabbatical. I flew back and forth to my sabbatical location during this time. They wanted me full time, but were willing to keep me on that basis than to lose me altogether. This allowed me to fund part of my sabbatical (while only being on sabbatical "part time") and get my feet wet in our new location.

Let's look at yet another scenario. You are single and in your late thirties and are very good at what you do, which is software design. But you are fed up with the corporate job marketplace and concerned that competition in your field (both in the country and offshore) will lessen your career prospects going forward. You have decided that you want to take your career into your own hands by starting a business – but you are not sure doing what. Most financially successful people are self-employed business owners or self-employed professional – so yours may be a very wise choice. Is it a risky one? Sure – many new businesses fail in their first few years. But look at it another way – is it not risky for you and your family to rely on the single source of income that a job provides?

You would start by asking yourself what it is you like about what you do. It could be helping to solve business problems with clever software, or you might gain satisfaction from training others in using your software to solve their problems. On the other hand it could be the art and craft of software engineering itself that has you in its sway. Or you might want to move away from software design but stay in the computer field. Perhaps you want to combine a love of writing with your love of technology and get into technical writing, which could mean writing articles or books, starting an online e-zine or blog, or other. Then again, maybe you want to move out of computing entirely.

If you have some ideas for what you want your business to accomplish, you are already on the way to planning a successful start-up. A successful business is always an intersection of value-added services (or of products) and a need, with a healthy dose of passion on the part of the business owner. If you are still unsure, or if your business plan lacks focus, you may want to concentrate your sabbatical on exploring the various options. But before jumping into the various exploratory sabbatical options, understand your personal goals.

Perhaps years of long days and nights designing software has left you with a nice nest egg but with severe damage to your social, family, and community life. You want to take time to build and nurture personal relationships, and maybe meet the right partner. You may want to consider volunteer work – either at home, or abroad with an organization like the Peace Corps or local volunteer organizations. Volunteers often "wear many hats," which will give you an opportunity to explore other types of jobs, recognize and develop other interests and skills, and perhaps even identify business opportunities. Volunteers working closely together for a cause they believe in can develop personal bonds that last a lifetime. And this is all on top of the spiritual satisfaction that you will achieve by helping others. If you will be volunteering close to home, you could even start to plan your business start-up while on sabbatical (once you know what you want to do). Business plans can be written and financing can be arranged while still on sabbatical.

Let's now look at the case of a mid-career manufacturing professional suddenly laid off from a mid or senior-level management job. This executive was only planning to work another ten years. But the reality that rapidly sets in is that in her field, there are fewer and fewer top management jobs available due to mergers and acquisitions, off-shoring of services and sourcing, and general cost-cutting. Moreover, there is blatant age discrimination whether acknowledged or not. From a personal standpoint, she had never thought about a sabbatical and though she wouldn't mind some free time and relaxation she is simply too nervous about not getting back into the job market quickly. Also, she is very satisfied with her work and cannot picture not doing what she does now. So what are her options – and how can a sabbatical (albeit a forced one) help?

She would like to share her experiences and consult to other manufacturers either as an independent consultant or as part of a professional services firm. Certainly she can approach the established services firms, but this forced sabbatical also offers the opportunity to explore independent consulting. So what she may consider, if her financial resources allow for it, is to spend some time making contacts, doing research, and writing papers on the topic. This time spent establishing herself as an "authority" can also be mixed with "fun." Why not fly out to San Francisco to meet with the head of an industry association, to Washington D.C. to treat a manufacturing lobbyist to a nice tax-deductible lunch, and so on? Make sure to mix in some well-deserved down time with the networking and research activities.

People in a creative profession have as much need for a sabbatical as anyone else. If you are a graphic artist, a musician, a writer, a dancer, and so on – and have been doing this for a fair number of years – then you know that you have your dry spells. How you deal with these dry spells and reawaken your artistic muse can determine how and if your career flourishes or dead-ends.

We have discussed people in a "knowledge" profession, and creative professionals. What about people in a more traditional product or service profession? This would include providers of home decorating services, painters, furnishings or antiques store owners, restaurant owners, grocers, auto-repair shop owners, insurance agents, and so on. The process of goal definition and mapping is no different here. Many antique store owners got into the field out of a love of history, cultures, art, or a particular region of the world; a sabbatical can be a perfect opportunity to feed that love and explore new avenues for business at the same time. An insurance agent may be burnt out trying to meet sales targets and may need the rest a sabbatical can promise; at the same time, they would like to increase sales in the future by breaking into a new ethnic market. A sabbatical in Asia may be a great way to reach out to Asian consumers afterwards.

There are as many sabbatical goals as there are people, and the intent here is not to attempt the impossible and list all possible scenarios. Instead, our focus is on showing how goals should be set by demonstration.

So much of the discipline and planning involved in organizing a sabbatical is identical for starting a business, and for leading a financially successful life even if you stay in an employee role. Living to a budget, putting together a plan, selling a proposal, learning to adapt to risk and changes, and prospering – these are the same attributes that most millionaires possess, according to the best-seller *The Millionaire Next Door*[2].

All we have been doing so far is talking about goals – the "what would I like to do" and the "what should I do to better myself and career." We have not yet discussed the effect that constraining factors of the financial resources at your disposal, and other personal and job factors would have (i.e., the "what can I do," "how can I do it," and "when").

Also, remember that this does not have to be a solitary exercise. Seek out others who have taken sabbaticals, listen to their stories, and ask lots of questions. Connect with organizations that offer fellowships or programs similar to the ones you are considering, and ask to speak with past participants. Hook up with groups that solicit volunteers, and talk to some of them.

Finally, look carefully at how you wrote down your goals. I bet that many of these start with the words "I'd like," "I want to," or "I should." That's fine for now. But when you finalize your proposal after homing in on your goals, alternatives, and financial plan – and after you build up your mind-set – you will find yourself changing this wording to "I will." That will reflect your confidence in yourself and in your plan to accomplish these goals.

4.3 Positioning

Before we go any further, consider how you will position your sabbatical. Positioning means how you will refer to your sabbatical experience in the future (think job interviews, meetings with potential clients, and even social settings). And the time to think about how this will be done is before you take the sabbatical – in fact, as you are setting your goals. And since you are still finalizing your goals, it is not too late to tweak them a bit to better position your sabbatical for later.

Why bother? Anyone who has ever come across a difficult hiring manager (I admit to being one myself) or client knows that when there are gaps in the resumes, the questions start. "What were you doing then?" "Were you fired, and did it take you that long to get another job? Why?" (And then the other questions form in the cynical interviewer's mind: "Was he in prison?" "Was she in rehab?"). Thinking about how to position your sabbatical when you return will help you finalize a good sabbatical plan. In other words, think first about what you want to present, then about how you might accomplish that goal.

You want to make sure that your sabbatical not only meets your goals, but also sounds like you enhanced your own marketability when you describe it later on. This is easier than it sounds.

If you spent time volunteering to help a developing country's new business owners to start up their ventures, think about how to sell this experience… You may have "consulted to small business owners to help them achieve such and such results." Or you may have "increased your cross-cultural awareness by working in a developing market." If you spent time resting and touring in another country, did you perhaps "achieve fluency is such and such language and gain intimate familiarity with that culture." Or if you did an adventure-travel experience, perhaps you "gained valuable experience in assessing and managing risks," "developed management and team-building skills by directing activities like…," or "developed greater situational awareness, resilience, resourcefulness, and flexibility by doing…"

Or will you start some sort of new venture during your sabbatical? Perhaps you will begin writing about what you do for a living, your hobby, or some other area in which you lend a unique and valued viewpoint? Writing is one of those amazing pursuits that can be done anywhere and everywhere. Freelancing as a model, photographer, journalist, musician, and so on is also possible anywhere. Or maybe you will use the opportunity to explore finally starting that business you've dreamed of. Freed of the normal day-to-day demands on your time, you can take time to explore your business strategy, conduct research, formulate a business plan, and so on. Or maybe you can use the sabbatical to "test drive" a career change, by taking volunteer, part-time, or junior work in an entirely different career. All of these show drive, ambition, and initiative (not to mention the technical skills attained in writing, planning a start-up company, and so on) and can be positioned strongly on your resume without much creative thought.

A sabbatical spent furthering your education can usually be positioned quite easily, especially where the learning is in an area that intersects with the type of work you typically do – or the type of work you would like to get into. Few would question the wisdom of someone who takes time off to go back to school, get an advanced degree or certification, or otherwise take classes that advance self and career.

Perhaps you wish to do volunteer work. See if you can emphasize the experience by delivering training or education or otherwise coaching people. If you will be doing the sabbatical through sponsorship of your company – or if you are planning to target a certain company upon your return in your job search – research the company's social responsibility goals (i.e., "pet causes") and determine whether your volunteering opportunity is in line with those goals. Or perhaps your volunteer assignment will involve acquiring language or cross-cultural skills, or new technical skills? Since there are often many volunteer alternatives, you should by all means select the one that lets you tell the best story in the future.

Remember that practically any sabbatical (if carefully planned) can be attractively positioned to employers and clients. That includes a sabbatical focusing on religious or spiritual growth. Think about some of the areas in which you will grow, and consider which would be of interest to someone contemplating paying you for a job. The sabbatical could "increase your ability to manage stress, handle pressure, and comfortably multitask," or it could make you "more self-directed and focused". The religious studies you undertake could "sharpen your research and debating abilities," and enable you to "make better arguments". Of course, if you can combine a spiritual/religious sabbatical with either or both volunteer work or international experience, you have an even better story to tell.

4.4 Priorities

Most of us have many goals – some lofty, some simple, some short-term, and others longer. We can't always get everything we want when we want it. It is also the case that if you try to do too much, you often end up accomplishing nothing. Therefore, we prioritize. Rank your goals according to three criteria – must do, want to do, and nice to do. "Must-do goals" are ones where if they are not met, you would call the sabbatical a failure. "Want-to-do goals" are those goals you would like to accomplish during the sabbatical, but if there is a group of them it is not disastrous if all of them are not met. Finally, "nice-to-do goals" are those goals that, if they can be accomplished during the sabbatical, your overall satisfaction increases; if they cannot, no big deal.

This should be done first after careful self-reflection, then after consulting those close to you. You will re-prioritize later, after you have assessed your resources, researched and priced sabbatical alternatives, and begun the planning process. But this first attempt at prioritization is your most personal and in a way most meaningful one.

Prioritizing your goals demands brutal honesty. If you have already tried to meet one of your must-do goals but failed, look at the reasons behind this failure. What lessons have you learned from that experience and what would you do differently this time to increase your chances of success? Perhaps you think it is time to reprioritize that goal for now and move on to other more achievable goals. There is no one answer to these questions; all I can do is guide you to ask them and encourage you to be forthright when answering yourself.

4.5 Success factors

When your mid-level goals are clear, you need to ask yourself how you will know when these goals are met. This is known as defining your success criteria. If your goals are specific, clear, and measurable, then this should not be hard. On the other hand, if you are having trouble determining when a goal has been reached, then it needs to be better thought out.

4.6 Generating sabbatical alternatives

Once you have an idea of what you want to do, you can evaluate sabbatical options. There are structured sabbaticals that tell you how long and what to do, and less structured ones that you design yourself. What I noticed when reading about others who have taken sabbaticals, they often presented either one person's story, or a sampling of sabbatical possibilities combined with a list of resources. But these lists were limited in scope, and were probably outdated soon after the books were published. Any list could not possibly encompass the ever-increasing alternatives for sabbaticals.

That is why the best way of researching alternatives is to first have an idea of what you want to do. By all means – read these other books, especially if you are confused about what you want to do and need some ideas. But the process of setting your goals should have you on the right track.

Also recognize that no one type of sabbatical is "better." If you or your sabbatical partners require a lot of structure, then a packaged sabbatical experience may be more comfortable for you. Certainly, a structured sabbatical is easier to plan and estimate costs for. However, as with taking a packaged tour versus planning your own vacation, there are benefits to a customized sabbatical in that you may have a closer fit to your own individual goals.

How do you go about generating ideas?

- Think about what you are searching for, and translate this into "search phrases" or what the denizens of the Internet call keywords. "Sabbatical" and "leave of absence" are effective but very general, and alone are likely to source good information about sabbaticals in general – but not as much about specific goals.
- To drill down to the specifics, think about your goals and try to translate them into fairly specific one to five-word search terms, such as "teach English in China," "volunteer in South Africa," "improve public speaking," "learn Arabic," "masters degree in interior design," "work in Paris," and so on. If your goals are still unclear but you have a target location in mind, you may want to search for "Sabbatical + Greece," for example.
- Do research in a library (a well-stocked metropolitan area library if possible) or bookstore. You should use the services of a good librarian in the case of a library, while in a bookstore you may want to check the travel, work (or work-life), or career section.
- Search the Internet (Web sites, discussion/interest groups, chat rooms, and so on) and online bookstores (http://www.amazon.com, http://www.bn.com, and others) using the search criteria you have developed above.
- The library or bookseller is also a good place to find updated career guides, travel books, lists of domestic and foreign universities, and so on.
- Communicate with people who have taken sabbaticals that appeal to you and seem consistent with your goals. Join online discussion groups or chat rooms dedicated to topics that mesh with your goals; most major discussion-group servers allow you to search for groups using search criteria.
- Talk to your family and trusted friends and get their initial feedback (make sure to let them know that you are only starting to look into this, and don't have a detailed plan yet).
- For a working sabbatical (more about that later), check the resources in the appendix. Many of the established online job-search portals can help you find jobs, part-time, or contract work (some of it even on a telecommuting basis) at home or abroad. There is an excellent portal for researching the right volunteer

opportunity also listed in the appendix.
- You may also want to speak with a career or work-life coach who has had experience with people with similar goals. But before committing to paying them, make sure to ask them to describe some of the others they have helped, and how they helped them.
- When evaluating specific sabbatical "programs," make sure to find out application criteria and deadlines, total cost, length of program, and start dates.
- Write down ideas, concerns, and other thoughts in a free-form manner; do not worry about what makes sense or not yet. A good time to do this is in a setting where you have plenty of time and quiet. For those with a family, this may mean getting out of the house and finding a quieter venue (even checking into a local hotel may be a good idea).

4.7 What will it cost?

For many, this is "the" question. How would you approach finding out the cost of a sabbatical? First, to the extent that the sabbatical will involve a pre-planned "program," those costs should be pretty clear. Make sure to determine what is included in those costs: program participation only, housing costs, full room and board, transportation costs, shipping costs? If yours will be a customized sabbatical, then you need to research what each element will cost. Use your expenses worksheet as a guideline: keep a copy of that worksheet with your current expenses filled in, but start a new one with your projections for monthly sabbatical expenses as well as one-off expenses like airfare, shipping, program fees, and so on. Then multiply by the amount of time you anticipate being on sabbatical (with some extra time built in to return from sabbatical and possible search for a job) to estimate overall sabbatical costs.

Also make sure to account for lost income during a sabbatical, living expenses, health-care costs, and lost pension accruals when looking at the true cost of a sabbatical. Remember that "sabbatical living expenses" and "normal living expenses" are two different things – so you will need separate expense worksheets for each. This is said not to scare you, but both to prepare you and also to encourage you to consider a working sabbatical, which we will soon discuss.

An excellent way of getting a benchmark figure for living costs is by letting the professionals do the research for you wherever possible. One of the best publicly available sources of this information is the

U.S. Government, who publishes *per diem* (daily) rates for many cities in the U.S. and around the world. These figures include the costs of meals, lodging, and other incidental expenses, and can be found at http://www.state.gov/m/a/als/prdm/ for non-U.S. locations and http://www.gsa.gov/Portal/gsa/ep/contentView.do?programId=9704 &channelId= – for U.S. locations. Keep in mind that these rates are on the high side particularly for lodging if you intend being in your destination for more than a month or two, since they are geared towards shorter term assignments and stays. Wherever you go, staying in a hotel beyond a month rarely makes economic sense, as rental housing is financially much more attractive. The same holds true for your sabbatical. The best bet to estimate longer term housing expense is to visit a local real-estate broker online.

Of course, when figuring the costs of a sabbatical you should also factor in any income you will be receiving during sabbatical. This includes any "passive" income like rental fees, investment returns, deferred income or bonuses, and the like, as well as any wages or salaries from a working sabbatical.

One conservative way to approach sabbatical financial planning is to budget for the same level of "income" over the sabbatical as beforehand. But to the extent that there may be a gap between the end of the sabbatical and finding other paid employment (and perhaps replenishing other funds spent), it is also a good idea to budget in some contingency funds. A good guideline is to plan 25% contingency. This means that if you are going on sabbatical for a year, plan on three months to readjust and find other work afterwards. If your cost estimate for the year is $60,000, plan on an overall budget of $75,000.

So will a sabbatical cost $10,000, $100,000, or something in between? It depends of course on how long your sabbatical will be, where it will take place, what you will be doing, whether it will be a working sabbatical or not, how many are accompanying you on sabbatical, and what your projected expenses will be while on sabbatical. But keep in mind that the average American wedding now costs nearly $30,000 (and that's just the average), that tuition at a private university can run that same amount per semester, and that financial requirements for retirement can stretch well into seven figures. We plan for these other events and we can plan for a sabbatical, too.

4.8 Evaluating the alternatives

Caveat emptor (buyer beware) is guidance to live by. Never rely on any of the materials we've just discussed to guarantee the right sabbatical, or indeed even a legitimate operation. Speak with people about the exact program you are looking into. Ask the program to provide references, and check them. Make sure any university or college you are planning to study in is accredited by the proper accreditation body. Remember that there is some amount of safety working for a "big name" company (a known multinational, a known language-teaching school, and so on), attending a "known" learning institution, volunteering for a recognized organization, etc. If you will be working for smaller, lesser known organizations (or even performing freelance work or tutoring to private individuals) make sure to clearly define and enforce payment terms. A tutor should be paid for lessons in advance, or at least after each session; failed payments or bounced checks should be resolved before any new sessions take place. Search the Internet and check with local regulators, chambers of commerce, or better business bureaus to see whether your "sabbatical partner" has had any complaints. The bottom line: do your due diligence on your sabbatical opportunity – whether you are fashioning it yourself, or selecting a ready-made program.

Also make sure you have generated more than a few alternatives, since some may not pass the "reality check" we will talk about next. Others may require an application procedure, and the unavoidable truth is that you may not be accepted.

Go back to your self-assessment. Make sure the goals you have set and the alternatives you are considering fit your reality. Are they likely to be acceptable to your partner and any family members joining you on sabbatical? Do (or can) they fit within your financial situation (though we will explore this more later)? Do they square with your personality, character, and background? Do they fit your reality of child-care or elder-care requirements? Don't spend too much time with alternatives that are obviously not feasible.

At this early stage in your sabbatical planning be careful not to discuss your plan too widely. It is still forming, and not yet ready for exposure to the criticism of the outside world. Keep the discussions with your own family, loved ones, and close friends, and those you fully trust and whose opinions you value. You should always avoid setting goals for yourself that actually reflect someone else's perceptions of you or desires for you – these reality-checking sessions can prompt those close to you to express these perceptions.

But don't get me wrong – to the extent that your plans will impact your loved ones – bring them into the discussion now rather than later. If an objective is to spend more time together as a family, and one solution is for you to work only part time during a working sabbatical, ask your family how this temporarily lower income will affect them in light of your being able to spend more time with them. If your objective is to relocate as a family to another location, discuss with them what this would mean to their lives. You may think you know what is important to them – but you may also be shocked. Talk – then listen.

5: Paying for It

5.1 The big picture

Accept that a sabbatical is going to cost you, as do all other life-changing events. Unless your employer offers you paid sabbatical time, you're going to have to take unpaid leave (or resign outright), or plan a working sabbatical whereby you work part of the time while on sabbatical. Some approach a sabbatical and justify the hit to their wallet with the thought that "I will be a better worker and much happier and focused, so I'll end up making much more money." That's great if it happens, but don't count on it. If anything, after a sabbatical you might decide you don't want to work as hard, or that you want to change your career to something less lucrative and more altruistic.

There is another way to look at this. If you are unwilling to compromise on the amount of money you make during your sabbatical, and perhaps for a period of time afterwards, this can mean that you give up the potential for much greater earnings later, especially if you use the sabbatical to make a major career shift into doing something you love.

If we all lived life "by the numbers," we would never take vacations or sabbaticals, would never have kids and would never do anything unnecessary that pinches our wallets. There are some things that money can't buy, and a sabbatical may be just what it takes for you to find it. Health, family, faith, community, friends, self-reliance, making dreams come true – all of these are the true keys to happiness and few can be acquired with money. Keeping this in mind will make financial planning for a sabbatical much easier.

How to finance a sabbatical is one of the most important challenges you need to meet. Rest assured that if you set your mind to this financial planning goal and stick to a plan with dedication, you can do it. But you must make saving and investing for your sabbatical a priority. Make the time to prepare and stick to a budget and financial plan, and you will find yourself with less to worry about before, and during, your sabbatical.

This is not a book about financial planning – there are many good ones in print. All I try to do is to present the basics for the sabbatical-taker. This means taking an assessment of your financial condition, knowing the cost of living in your sabbatical destination, estimating other sabbatical costs, setting a financial target, and preparing and keeping to a sabbatical budget in order to meet that target. And as this is not a book about tax planning, all I will do is help you discover the right questions to ask of your tax advisors. You should be encouraged and probably surprised to find out that you can get tax breaks for going on sabbatical, to the extent that you will engage in business while on sabbatical! (Isn't that working sabbatical sounding better and better?) You may be able to deduct business expenses for travel, lodging, and meals, earn a foreign earned income exclusion, and deduct expenses associated with renting your house. But this is a tricky area (especially if your sabbatical destination is outside of your home country/economic zone), so make sure to consult a tax advisor who is licensed to give tax advice in both countries.

The bottom line is that you can build up a fund for your sabbatical in a few different ways: selling assets, increasing or maintaining income (during or prior to sabbatical), obtaining grants/scholarships/gifts, or taking on additional liabilities like loans. In any case, I strongly recommend setting up a separate savings account for your sabbatical fund. It is easier to measure your savings progress against your goal that way, and you should be less tempted to dip into these funds for other purposes.

That account could be a simple money-market account, or a brokerage account split into cash and a short-term portfolio of fixed-income investments and equity funds. Playing the market to try and grow the sabbatical fund quicker is an option for the experienced investor, but is not without risk.

5.2 Work

I strongly advocate financing a sabbatical by taking a working sabbatical. Part of all of the costs of the sabbatical that you had estimated in the last chapter can be defrayed by working while on sabbatical. An alternative is convincing your current employer to sponsor you.

5.3 Other increased income

Another way of financing a sabbatical is by earning extra income prior to taking the sabbatical. Perhaps you work at a job where you have the option of working extra hours or weekends for extra pay. Or, if you own your own business, you may be able to take on more business. If these options are not open to you, perhaps you can "moonlight," and work on the evenings or weekends separately from your job, as long as your primary employer allows this.

Can you bring in extra rental income by renting your primary or vacation home before you go away? (You may want to do this during your sabbatical as well). Ask yourself another question – is a sabbatical important enough to you to sacrifice some of your standard of living a year or two in advance by paying lower housing costs for a smaller or otherwise less expensive home? Keep in mind that a $500 difference in rent per month adds up to $6,000 towards your sabbatical fund after a year and $12,000 after two years! (Though this rental income is likely to be taxable, any expenses you incur to improve your home for renting it and for managing the rental are likely to be tax deductible – check with your tax advisor.)

5.4 Grants

You may be able to apply for a grant or a scholarship to defray your sabbatical costs, particularly if your goals include research, continuing education, or volunteer work for a specific cause. If you are investigating specific packaged sabbatical programs, ask whether they offer these incentives, or at least financial aid. The appendix contains some resources to help you get started looking for these, but never forget that your Web browser and search portal are potent tools here as well.

In some cases family or friends may offer you some financial support. This may be a touchy subject, and is best broached after you have your plan together. (Not surprisingly, even family will feel better about supporting a well thought-out idea).

Finally, you may want to approach your community about sabbatical support, to the extent that your sabbatical goals may be of interest to them. For example, if you plan on volunteering with needy people at home or abroad, your local religious or social institutions may be in a position to collect and provide you with support to do so. You may want to solicit Internet contributions if you intend to pursue a hobby or personal passion, and promise to report on it and reply to questions via your Web site. If you are contemplating spending time researching how microfinance is helping farmers in India, you may be able to approach an international bank and offer to share your findings with them if they can support your research. On the other hand, if you actually work for an international bank, then approaching them is more likely to be successful in the context of full sponsorship of your sabbatical.

5.5 Increase savings/reduce expenses

One of the simplest ways to finance a sabbatical is by reducing discretionary expenses and routing the money into savings for a period of time before the sabbatical. We've all heard about the "latte effect," whereby skipping that daily $4 latte and saving or investing the money instead can reap big rewards over time. But though this is a good long-term principle, we have to go further faster. Go through your expenses worksheet, credit card bills, and bank statements and put a tick mark next to each category that you consider discretionary. Normally this would include things like eating out, entertainment, consumer electronics, vacations, spa visits, other "lifestyle" purchases, and the like. At one level, anything other than food, clothing, shelter, and arguably education is a candidate for consideration. But even these core categories don't come in just one flavor: there are many housing options at different costs, many more clothing choices, and so on.

Go through the list and see:

- What can be eliminated (the annual vacation this year)?
- What can be cut or reduced (visits to the spa; restaurant meals)?
- What can be substituted for (cheaper housing; changing to a less expensive schooling option, at least temporarily)?

Scour your list of expenses in this manner, cut a little bit here and a little bit there, and plan to divert that extra money towards your new sabbatical savings account.

Pay attention to your automatic teller machine (ATM) withdrawals. Look at how much cash you withdrew and what you spent it on. Could you have withdrawn less? What about credit card and loan fees and expenses – can you consolidate credit cards, car loans, and other high interest debt to a lower debt service expense? Or can you use parts of your portfolio that are yielding less than the debt (for example, money in low-yielding money market or bond funds) to pay off higher-interest debt? Once you are free of debt, try to stay that way – only purchase what you have cash for.

We already mentioned that relocating or downsizing can save you money on your monthly housing expense. But the savings can go much further than that: if you live in an area with a high cost of living, moving to a less expensive area saves not only on your mortgage payment, but in less obvious places like the cost of heating, cooling, insuring, and repairing your home, property taxes, etc. You can sock all the savings away for your sabbatical or also use some for retirement. What else can you downsize – an extra car, private-school tuition, club memberships?

5.6 Sell assets

Another source of sabbatical financing is selling off some of your assets. Whether it is a watch, jewelry, painting, collections, or other valuables, you may want to consider selling some of those that do not hold sentimental value. This could even include your car if you don't need it during your sabbatical. Or maybe it's time to tap into the equity that has built up in your home by selling it.

Still, tread carefully when considering the sale of home or car. Make sure you know where you will get the money from to buy a replacements when it's time to reenter the workforce from sabbatical. If you have taken a lot of time off, it may be harder to get a loan before you have held onto a new job for a period of time. Also, you should check the latest tax laws with sales of primary residences since it may be that your profits could be subject to capital gains tax if you do not buy a new residence within a set amount of time.

Another route is selling some of your investment assets – stock, mutual funds, bonds, and so on. Or you could tap into your savings – but be sure to leave an emergency fund of at least three to six months of living expenses (don't use your last dollar). Consult a licensed tax planner first. In some cases, it may be better not to do this all before you go on sabbatical, but to do at least some of this while on sabbatical (to take your gains in a year with less income may mean paying less taxes). You may be subject to capital gains tax, but timing the sale may allow you to reduce or at least spread your tax liability over more than one year.

5.7 Loans

Loans come in many flavors. You might decide to take a loan against the cash values of your life insurance policy, or to cash in an annuity. (Before you do so, however, find out about the surrender charges. That includes any mutual funds that have back-end loads.) You may consider taking a home equity loan or reverse mortgage, a personal loan, or even some money from credit cards (beware the higher interest rates though). To the extent that you have or are starting a business, you may be able to obtain a business loan if you can show that your sabbatical will satisfy a business purpose.

You may want to draw on some money from a retirement plan (either via a loan or a distribution of funds). If you do, make sure not to raid the entire fund, and also beware the difference on your tax liability between a loan and a distribution. Under U.S. tax law for example, an early distribution from a (contributory occupational pension) 401 (k) retirement plan carries a 10% penalty, plus you get taxed at ordinary income rates on the amount of money you take out. Alternatively, if your company will give you a leave of absence instead of making you quit, you probably can borrow from your pension plan without paying this penalty. Remember, though, that if you don't go back to that company and your employment status is terminated, your loan must be paid back to the pension plan immediately. Countries that have similar type plans (Canada, with its Registered Retirement Savings Plan, RRSP, and Australia's superannuation plans) also allow for taxable early withdrawal or loans. Early pension release in the U.K. however is only possible if you are at least 50 years old – so other sources of financing are necessary here. This is generally the case throughout Europe, as the often publicly funded pension schemes (in contrast with the Commonwealth nations' schemes of employer plus employee funding) do not allow its beneficiaries to borrow or withdraw pension money early.

If you will be applying for a loan to fund your sabbatical, be sure to do so before you actually leave employment to go on sabbatical. If you are on unpaid leave, it's going to be harder.

5.8 Insurance

No discussion about sabbatical financial planning would be complete without mention of insurance. What do you need to know about insurance and sabbaticals? In this discussion, we assume that you already have the basic insurance protection in place – health, life insurance, disability insurance, homeowner's insurance (if you own a home) and auto insurance. You may also have umbrella liability coverage, long-term care insurance, dental insurance, or separate insurance coverage if you own a business.

How much of this insurance coverage is your own, and how much is via your employer? If you have successfully negotiated for an employer-sponsored sabbatical, will they offer to continue your insurance? If not, you should plan on acquiring your own insurance policies – you should never go without insurance coverage even during sabbatical. One option in the U.S. is to take advantage of the law known as "COBRA," whereby you can continue your work insurance policies by paying the employer's premium cost for up to 18 months after you leave your job. If you are fortunate enough to live in a land with some level of nationalized insurance coverage, then you can probably rely on this coverage during your sabbatical (but do check whether this coverage applies if you spend any significant time abroad).

But – wherever you live – check with your insurance providers whether your travel plans for your sabbatical will have any impact on your coverage. Since you are not planning to relocate (at least, not at this point), it is likely that your trip will be viewed as vacation travel and there should be no impact on your coverage. However, depending upon the activities you are planning to do and where you plan to do them, there may be issues. In particular, read the fine print of your health insurance, disability, and life insurance policies to see whether you are covered in foreign countries for things like medical services, hospitalization, disability suffered while overseas, or death overseas. If there is any doubt, check with the insurance company or your insurance agent.

5.9 Tax considerations

5.9.1 DEDUCTIBILITY OF BUSINESS EXPENSES

In many developed economies including the U.S., business expenses for a trip (domestic or international), which is primarily focused on business are tax deductible. In the U.S., the trip needs to be less than one year and you need to maintain your primary residence in the U.S. (see relevant Internal Revenue Service (IRS) Publications).

For U.S. tax purposes, travel expenses are the "ordinary and necessary" expenses of traveling away from home for your business, profession, or job. An ordinary expense is one that is common and accepted in your field of trade, business, or profession. A necessary expense is one that is helpful and appropriate for your business. There are similar provisions allowing for the deductibility of travel and related subsistence expenses in the tax codes of many other developed countries, including the U.K. and Canada.

First of all, if you leave town, travel, lodging, meals, and other incidentals are deductible (within certain limits) as a business expense. The price you pay for enjoying this incentive is having to keep excellent records to substantiate every such expense and being able to demonstrate, if audited, that the sabbatical was a legitimate professional activity, not education, nor a vacation. And above all, the key is to make sure that your trip can be viewed as a business trip. Think back to the goals of your trip – can these goals be "tweaked" such that some sort of business becomes a primary focus? Be careful, and consult a tax advisor before expecting to deduct business expenses. And if changing your goals just to lower your tax liability makes your sabbatical unattractive, then you should think twice.

5.9.2 AVOIDING DOUBLE INCOME TAXATION

Most countries only tax you for income earned within its borders – not so the United States. Citizens and residents residing and working abroad for decades are still liable for taxes. But the U.S. recognizes that forcing its citizens to pay U.S. and local national taxes would effectively cripple its ability to compete internationally, so it has signed tax treaties with most major trading partners to eliminate double income taxation by agreement of the two nations.

What if a U.S. citizen or resident plans to stay away more than a year? Up to $80,000 of foreign income (at the time of this writing) can be excluded from federal income tax if you stay away that long. This is called the "Foreign Income Exclusion." To qualify, the worker must be out of the United States for at least 330 full days over a period of 12 consecutive months.

This helps make up for the fact that the cost of living in many foreign capitals may be higher than it is at home. A two-income couple could conceivably qualify for up to $160,000 of exclusion. "Unearned" income doesn't count, such as dividends, interest, alimony, pension payments, and most rental income. If you are away less than a year, ordinary and necessary business expenses are deductible. If you go away for more than a year and elect to use the Foreign Income Exclusion, your expenses are only deductible proportionate to the amount of income you earn above the maximum exclusion.

In addition to your sabbatical salary potentially being tax sheltered, the rules allow for a "Foreign Housing Deduction and Exclusion," which may be of additional benefit. Tax treaties between the United States and most foreign countries generally exempt from foreign tax the wages of American professors teaching and conducting research abroad. But even if you do work that is taxable in the foreign country, this can be a credit or a deduction on your U.S. tax form.

5.9.3 RENTING YOUR HOME

Renting your house out while you're gone can be quite favorable from a tax perspective, as everything associated with the home becomes a business expense. There's a lot of risk in bringing strangers into your home, so a good rental agent is worth paying for and is deductible. Under the right conditions, you can deduct more than the value of the rental income, so some people take that opportunity to throw in some repairs that would have to be done eventually. All of the costs of upkeep, many of which you would otherwise have to pay without the deductibility, become deductible while the house is rented, and you get to deduct depreciation.

5.9.4 CHARITABLE CONTRIBUTIONS

A sabbatical can be a great excuse to do the "mother of all spring cleanings." If you will be paying to store your belongings, the less you have to store, the less you will pay. Consider giving some of these away to charity. Not only will you be doing a good deed, many nations offer tax deductibility of approved charitable contributions. That way, your following year tax position will be even brighter. (Yes, a tax refund is also a source of sabbatical financing!)

5.10 Travel insurance/medical assistance

Do you need any additional insurance if you will be traveling or staying outside of your normal location (even outside the country) during your sabbatical? You may want to consider travel health insurance, which provides coverage for you during the various stages of your travels. But, as with any new insurance policy, check the fine print for any conditions or exclusions. Some travel policies have an age limit, and many will not cover you for any pre-existing medical conditions.

Medical Assistance Programs are not insurance in the strict sense, but these can be invaluable particularly when traveling abroad. These help you locate doctors and hospitals abroad (particularly useful when you are familiar with neither the local health-care system nor the language) and can arrange for a medical evacuation to your home country in the event of a serious medical condition (or arrange for your remains to be returned home in the event of death). Since these programs are not insurance, they do not cost nearly as much. The appendix has some resources for locating travel insurance and medical assistance providers.

5.11 Providing for the worst

Sabbatical or not – if others depend on you, you need a will. Even if not, chances are that you don't want your assets distributed by the government after your passing. The safest route to creating a will is by making an appointment with a local lawyer who specializes in wills and estate planning. Besides a will, you should make sure that you have named beneficiaries to your insurance policies and investments.

5.12 General budgeting guidelines

What makes a good budget? First, make sure that you don't simply select the categories just discussed (or those in any financial planning book) – they may not all be relevant to you. Make sure the categories fit your own financial situation, not this generic picture.

Keep a detailed record of your monthly expenses for six months, subtracting out work-related costs (such as dry cleaning, lunches out, commuting costs) and adding in the projected extra costs of your sabbatical plans (such as travel, home renovation, and so on). Don't forget to also add in expenses that your employer pays now but that you will have to pay if you take a leave of absence or quit (such as medical expenses). Multiply your monthly basic expenses times the number of months you plan to be on sabbatical, and add in the extra costs of your sabbatical activities. Unless you will have a guaranteed job waiting for you upon your return, add at least three extra months for job hunting just to be safe.

Next, make sure to be realistic in your budget. If you project that you will make extra income in the upcoming year (perhaps you expect a raise, a larger bonus, more overtime, or you expect to take on an additional job or freelance work) then make sure your projections are accurate and conservative. Make the opposite assumption with expenses – always build in a buffer for unforeseen expenses, and overestimate any expenses that aren't fully known (home repair or renovation, medical work, and so on). If you tend towards underestimating income and overestimating expenses, then at worst you should not be too disappointed if your pessimism is warranted; at best, you will be pleasantly surprised with higher than forecast net income.

Finally, make sure you know how to – and intend to – track your income, spending, savings, and investments according to your budget. After all, your budget is a financial plan to let you take the sabbatical of your dreams – embrace it!

If this all seems daunting, you may want to engage a financial planner to help you. Remember, you are interviewing a potential financial planner so be prepared with the right questions.

- Ask the financial planner to describe their planning approach. This explanation should be understandable to you even if you are not a financial professional. If it is not, then either they are not sufficiently familiar with their subject or they communicate poorly!
- Would you be working with them alone, or with a team? If the latter, make sure to review the backgrounds of the team members as well.
- Do they have a good financial and educational background, and licensing as a financial planner? Degrees in business, accounting, finance, or the like are preferred. Preferably, this financial planner should have a number of years of experience in the field.
- Do they have an existing network of other financial and legal professionals with whom they work when additional or specialist expertise is required?
- Describe your sabbatical goals to the financial planner, and an overview of your current financial condition. Ask about their experience helping other clients plan for early or mid-life events (sabbaticals or otherwise). Make sure to relate your needs and goals to the experience of the financial planner.
- The financial planner should be comfortable providing references.
- How does the financial planner intend to work with you? How much of your and their time is required?
- How will he or she work with you to monitor your progress on your financial plan?

Make sure they describe their fee structure, and that it is clear and acceptable to you.

6: The Working Sabbatical

6.1 What in the world...?

Before we move away from goal definition, I want to introduce the idea of a "working sabbatical." Wait a minute – is it a sabbatical if you are still working? Let's think about this. Is rest and relaxation absolutely counter to the concept of work? Maybe, or at least to the type or amount of work you are doing right now. But would it not be relaxing and fulfilling alike to do or learn about the work you've always dreamed of on sabbatical? You see, the essence of a sabbatical is not just rest but change and growth: change from your routine, change from your surroundings, new goals, and a plan to grow because of them. If the work you take on during your sabbatical facilitates this, then a working sabbatical is no contradiction in terms.

First let us make a distinction between a sabbatical and other "work-life" measures like flextime, compressed working schedules, part-time work, and remote teleworking. In fact, a working sabbatical often has elements of both of the latter two. These work-life devices usually are recommended to fill the same types of needs as a sabbatical. However, such arrangements often involve the same type of work and company, and the same surroundings, such that the only change is to the work schedule and load – allowing you some extra time for the rest of your life. And as we have said, if your major challenge is fitting the rest of your life into your working schedule, such measures may be the answer for you. If you are in need of other changes, or deeper rest and renewal, then these work-life measures usually do not go far enough.

In the end, the fact of your doing work matters less to your sabbatical than whether there is actual rest, change, and growth. If your current job agrees to keep you on as a consultant on a retainer basis for one year, putting in five to eight days a month, this may help you do the things you want, relax, and instigate the changes in your life you crave. If you have been fantasizing about living and working in France and your company offers to transfer you to its offices there, is this a working sabbatical? If the offer also entails a reduced work schedule – at least for a significant period of time – then perhaps it is a very exciting sabbatical offer. If you will be working a full schedule, then although there will be change involved, there will be little scope for rest – so this is best thought of as an international assignment rather than a sabbatical.

A working sabbatical does not, though, mean that you need stay with your current company. You may decide to take a part-time job teaching English abroad, or using your skills in a consulting or teaching capacity. If you own your own business, you may use your sabbatical to drum up business in a new market or location or to learn about other products, services, or markets that could be relevant to you.

The best way to approach thinking about a working sabbatical is to formulate a project that you can accomplish on your sabbatical that can help achieve the working goals you have set for yourself. Remember the personal/career goal-mapping exercise we discussed earlier – a working sabbatical is one particularly powerful implementation of this. Think about things that would help your career:

- Writing a book or a series of articles
- Meeting clients/competitors
- Doing market research directly in a new market
- Learning other skills, crafts, arts, and techniques at the source or with a master practitioner
- Learning other languages
- Immersion in a culture that is or will become important to your company or business
- Meeting and spending time with other colleagues
- Going back to school

6.2 Finding work

The best way to find work is, and has always been, through personal connections. If you know people in the area you are seeking work, check first with them to see if they are aware of opportunities. Next, check through any industry affinity groups, unions, professional associations, or networking groups (career, social, or religious) you belong to. A chamber of commerce in the area you are planning to take your sabbatical can also point you in the right direction. Also check employment agencies and recruiters, and local newspapers, in the area you are targeting for your sabbatical – remember that not all jobs are posted to the Internet. Finally, the Internet job boards are popular places to start. Many of the larger ones have full-time, part-time, and contract job listings in many geographies and fields. Some even specialize in telecommuting jobs. The appendix has a representative list of these job boards.

Keep in mind that the individual doing the hiring would much rather hire someone they know. In much of the world, in fact, a business owner would really prefer to hire a relative or friend who needs the money rather than an unknown individual from the other side of the world. The exception to this is where only a foreigner or someone with special skills can do the job (such as a certified "English as a second language" teacher, or someone with specialist skills). In some cultures, it will be possible to arrange work before you arrive at your destination; in others (Israel is a good example), you will be regarded as a complete unknown until you are present and accounted for. And you will need to convince a potential employer that you are likely to stay around long enough to provide benefit to them. They will be naturally wary of foreigners who may up and leave at any time, leaving them in the lurch.

Job-hunting resources change constantly, and Internet job boards disappear, merge, or lose importance. A recently written career search book (particularly one directed at the area or country you are targeting for your sabbatical) can help keep you on track. The online booksellers (such as http://www.amazon.com and http://www.bn .com) often have these most recent titles if your local bookstore does not.

If you are planning a sabbatical in another country, teaching English is an excellent way to meet the locals, earn money, and make connections. The appendix has a list of some well-known schools that are always seeking English teachers. Either way, focus your search on the large cities, which are likely to have a greater demand for these services. Also, a targeted search of the major online booksellers will yield titles for teaching English as a second language, and many titles geared to English teaching in specific countries like Japan, France, and so on.

Part of the beauty of a sabbatical lies in its unpredictability. No matter if you have arranged your working sabbatical opportunity up front or not, there are likely to be opportunities that come your way once you are in your destination, just by dint of your background, language skills, and nationality – particularly if you know or are learning the local language. Keep an open mind and you may be pleasantly surprised at what happens. Remember that your first sabbatical job is not necessarily your last.

When you spend time in one place, you get a chance to form bonds and meet people who can help you. As someone who has lived abroad, I can attest to the fact that the expatriate population is a small community; becoming part of it leads to many fun, interesting, and productive contacts. Make an effort, and become a part of this community. Of course, networking makes the most sense if you will be in one place long enough during your sabbatical.

6.3 Remote working

One way to balance the income you can receive from a working sabbatical with the need for time off to relax is via "remote working." Remote working – also known as teleworking or telecommuting – involves using technology to work from home or an alternate convenient location, rather than commuting or traveling to a workplace. There are remote workers in many organizations – spending some, most, or all of their time working from their homes. Similarly, many freelancers and those who operate businesses from their homes practice remote working.

This type of working is enabled by technologies like computers, high-speed Internet connections, wireless computing, instant messaging, videoconferencing, mobile phone technologies with advanced call forwarding/"follow me" capabilities, voicemail, virtual fax numbers, secure virtual private networks into an organization's central information network, "on-demand" office space with conference room facilities and secretaries, and so on. The object is to bring the office to you by replicating the capabilities of a fully outfitted office, even if you are sitting on the beach with your wireless laptop and mobile phone.

Remote working can be feasible for work that requires thinking, information processing, and writing – data analysis, tax and accounting analysis and preparation, reviewing grants or cases, writing; and telephone-intensive tasks – setting up a conference, obtaining information, following up on participants in a study. Remote working also works well for computer-oriented tasks – programming, Web page design, network administration and support, data entry, and word processing, and so on.

Remote working is harder where face-to-face contact is a job requirement – as in many service industries, health care, public service, and so on. But harder does not always mean impossible. If you are in one of these industries, can you write about what you do, your industry, and so on? Articles for magazines and trade journals, blogs or even a book can be a valued source of income and a nice supplement and enhancement to your career. Or you may be able to provide online consultancy for what you do. And if you are working in food service, child care, or the like – you may mistakenly think that no one is interested in hearing your stories and perspective. But don't you have humorous, interesting, or even incredible stories to tell? Remember – not only "knowledge workers" have experience or stories to write or consult about.

6.4 Work visa

If you are looking into a working sabbatical outside of your country or economic zone, you are likely to need a work visa. The best place to understand the requirements is that country's embassy or Web site. In some cases, the job you are seeking could arrange visa sponsorship for you. Or you may be able to get a work visa by promising to start a business, do research for your existing business or company, and so on. Having a current connection with a company based in that country can certainly help.

7: Employer Sponsorship

Employer sabbatical sponsorship is an aspiration for those who seek the confidence of knowing that their job is secure, or that some of their compensation or benefits may be paid during the sabbatical. Yet before checking into this option, you should regard this as merely one sabbatical alternative. That is to say you should have one or two alternate plans that do not involve employer sponsorship. As we will see, this is because such sponsorship is not always common, not easily obtained, and might not meet with your sabbatical goals. But when you can get it, it can make your sabbatical planning much smoother. Having alternate sabbatical plans and financing sources will also help you exude more confidence when negotiating a sponsorship plan with your employer.

7.1 The law

There is no law in any nation that I'm aware of that guarantees sabbaticals (smaller, limited pilot programs in Finland and Sweden aside), though there are shorter-term protections for specific purposes. The U.S. Family and Medical Leave Act of 1993 (FMLA), for example, provides up to 12 weeks of unpaid, job-related leave each year under specific circumstances to U.S. employees of public agencies or private firms of more than 49 people. These circumstances include the following:

- To take care of an immediate family member – specifically, a parent, spouse or child – who has a serious health condition
- To take care of yourself if you have a serious health condition of your own
- To take care of your newborn baby in the weeks after the child is born
- To take care of a child you've adopted in the weeks after the child arrives in your midst

When you take leave under the this Act, you can do so knowing that the law requires your employer to assign you to your old job when you return or, at the very least, to an equivalent job with equivalent pay, benefits, and other terms and conditions of employment, according to the U.S. Department of Labor (DOL). Your employer is also required to maintain group health insurance coverage for you, assuming you had such coverage before your leave. Almost 24 million American workers took advantage of the law between January 1999 and October 2000, according to the most recent DOL figures.

To learn more about the FMLA, check out these DOL resources:

- http://www.dol.gov/elaws/esa/fmla/
- http://www.dol.gov/asp/programs/guide/fmla.htm

Britain has had national maternity leave legislation since 1978, with coverage expanded to all working women in 1993 to bring the United Kingdom into compliance with the European Union's (EU's) parental-leave directives. These allow at least three months of leave to mothers and fathers up until the child is eight years old. Most EU nations go much further than the U.K. – France is a good example. French law entitles all employees, men and women, to take parental leave of up to one year or to work part-time following the birth or adoption of a child up until the child's third birthday (or anniversary of adoption). This leave is renewable; after the first year, employees may either extend their leave or part-time work, or switch from leave to part-time work. The leave is unpaid, but eligible employees receive a state allowance for their second and subsequent children. At the end of the leave or part-time work, employees return to their previous job or a similar job with the same salary.

7.2 Company sabbatical policies

In the U.S. there are limited-term sabbatical-leave policies at roughly 10% of firms, according to recent surveys. These provide for an average of one to three month sabbaticals, usually with some level of pay and benefits. A much smaller sample of employers have offered six month sabbaticals or longer, or sabbaticals in exchange for pay rollbacks.

Like any employee benefit, sabbatical programs can be cut back or eliminated at an employer's whim. So it is fair to say that if what you are looking for is a real (longer and more rewarding) sabbatical, you may need to look beyond these programs. But what you can do is negotiate with your employer to try to get them to "sponsor" your sabbatical. This could mean many things like: keeping your job open for your return, paying you full or part salary while on sabbatical, providing full or partial benefits on sabbatical, continuing your tenure in pension or other accumulating benefit plans, and so on. The company may ask nothing in return, or it may set certain conditions for you to meet prior to, during, or following your sabbatical upon return to work. We will explore these later.

7.3 Know the score

Knowing your employer's position on sabbaticals can help you to determine how and if they will support your sabbatical. Here's a list of areas to look into to find out more:

- When you were hired, was a sabbatical or leave of absence part of your compensation package or contract?
- Is there a sabbatical policy (check your employee handbook, human resources department)?
- Is there a "work-life" policy that allows for time off, flex-time, part-time, remote working, job-sharing, compressed workweeks, or the like?
- Regardless of policy – have actual sabbaticals been approved to your knowledge?
- Listen to the grapevine – the best source of news in most organizations. Have sabbatical applications been declined, and if so, why? (Try to talk to those who've been approved and those who've been declined.)
- If there is a policy, are you eligible for a sabbatical?
- Is there an unofficial policy?
- Does the company culture support the idea of a sabbatical?
- Who would be able to approve a sabbatical?
- Can you negotiate directly with them or do you need to go through your line manager or other gatekeepers?
- Do the approvers have any "pet causes" or agendas?
- If leaves or sabbaticals have been granted, to whom?
- Do they share any common characteristics (rank in the organization, tenure, department, or other common identifier)?
- How were their absences dealt with during their sabbaticals?
- Aside from your company, what do the competitors and others in your industry do regarding sabbaticals?
- What is the general economic health of your company?

- Does your job involve any slow or very busy times that should be borne in mind when planning a sabbatical?

Further to the above, you need to understand your employer's standpoint. As most employers share common concerns about sabbaticals, be familiar with what they are so that you can assure them that they do not apply in your case!

- "If we let you go, everyone else will want to go too!" (Any organization should have a policy that prevents too many critical employees from taking sabbatical simultaneously – as a matter of common sense!)
- "Won't this create more work for your manager and colleagues?" (Assure them that you will train a replacement, provide some support after you are gone, and return ready to take on an even-larger workload!)
- "Won't it be expensive supporting you on sabbatical – between health care, salary, lost productivity, other benefits?" (Negotiate!)
- "What if you don't come back?" (Assure them that you will, and that you will be even more ready to take on new challenges. Let them know that if any employees do not return after a sabbatical, then the organization would have lost them eventually anyway since their heart was not into their work.)

As we will see, you will have to seize the bull by the horns and sell the idea to higher management and human resources – rather than looking to them for solutions.

7.4 Establish your value – and your flexibility

Educate your employer and show why a sabbatical will make business sense for them. Whether or not your organization has a formal sabbatical policy, you must present your case in the form of a proposal. This should make clear the sabbatical overview (details including what, why, when, how long, and where), the benefits to you and to the organization, the costs of the sabbatical, the risks to the organization and how you propose they be mitigated.

Let your employer know that you are willing to be flexible. It is too easy to say "no" to a sabbatical request especially if it is new for them, so don't give them any excuses. Be flexible about the time frame – don't ask for six months off at the same time your company plans to launch an important project. You may want to be flexible about doing some work during your sabbatical (providing that it allows you to meet your own goals, of course). Offer to train someone to cover your job while you're gone.

7.5 Your proposal

Keep in mind that your goals, and what your employer would want out of a sabbatical, may be different. When drawing up a proposal, figure out what your employer may like you to come out of a sabbatical with – improved language or cultural skills, building a relationship with key customers or suppliers in your sabbatical region, exploring business or investment opportunities in your sabbatical region, learning new technical skills, improving your teaching/coaching/communicating skills, and so on.

In a sense, this process is not too different from interviewing for a job. You have your own goals and wants out of the job, and the employer has theirs. The trick is finding an intersection between these, and then selling your case so that you meet your goals and they meet theirs. This is an extension of the goal-mapping technique you learned earlier. But now we bring a third source of goals into the mix, supplementing your personal and career goals – those goals of your employer.

Frankly, your employer could hardly care about your deep-seated need for a sabbatical. (OK, maybe some bosses do really care...) At any rate, your employer is mainly bothered by "what's in it for them." That's fine – make your sabbatical proposal speak to that.

In your proposal, try to present two or three alternatives, "value adds", to your organization. Realize that any proposal is just the starting point to a dialogue and negotiations. As these discussions move further along, be aware of your "breaking point." That is the point where what your employer wants out of you is so different to what you want out of the sabbatical that you no longer want their sponsorship. Having a few alternative proposals (all consistent with your goals) is one way to prevent this from happening.

The starting point is to research, from the organization's perspective, the business problems that you can help solve through your sabbatical. Following are examples of possible key challenges. Let's see how this might work by looking at some of these typical organizational challenges, and the skills or objectives you can develop while on sabbatical that can help the organization meet these challenges.

Organizational challenge	Intersecting sabbatical goals
New markets	Language skills Cultural skills Advanced education Out-of-the-box thinking Targeted work experience
New technologies and methods	Technology skills training Advanced education Self-directed research
Keeping up with workload	Limited remote working Train replacement worker Document procedures and tools Leadership skills through volunteering, adventure sabbaticals Problem-solving skills Risk-management skills
Organizational change	Cost management and budgeting skills Change-management skills Risk-management skills People skills Communication skills

New products/services	Developing creative, out-of-the-box
	  thinking through a travel and
	  adventure sabbatical
	Onsite market research
	Advanced education

7.6 Proposal guidelines

First, use clear, simple language and stick to the facts. Emotional appeals, including claims to entitlement – at least in a written proposal – are not businesslike and will not help your organization make a decision in your favor. "After eleven years of hard work for the company I deserve this sabbatical" should be scrapped; instead, focus on the accomplishments you had in these eleven years, and those you hope to achieve during and when you return from sabbatical. Avoid exaggeration and stick to facts and reasonable projections. Your sabbatical will indeed be an amazing, life-changing, deeply emotional experience but you don't need to tell that to your boss (who can probably guess that anyway); keep your proposal businesslike. And, regardless of whether your sabbatical plan is simple or not, you should not over complicate your proposal by including every last detail. Focus on:

- Where you will be
- What you will be doing
- What you can accomplish that can help your organization
- How long you plan to do this for
- What your transition and risk-management plan is

Secondly, make sure to address how this sabbatical arrangement will work with clients/patients, users, colleagues, management, and other stakeholders. These points would include:

- When and how will you inform and prepare them of your sabbatical plans
- Who will cover for you while you are away
- How they will be trained and prepared to do so
- How or if you can be contactable in emergencies
- How you will keep in touch during your sabbatical
- How your sabbatical will affect your co-workers, and what can be done to minimize the impact of your leave on them and the organization (talk about it with trusted co-workers)

Then be sure to have it clear in your mind regarding the following points and make sure you know your "bottom line" and priorities on:

- Timing of sabbatical
- Content of sabbatical
- Length of time away
- Compensation
- Benefits during sabbatical
- Return path into the organization
- Willingness to say in touch or perform some limited work duties during the sabbatical
- Willingness to give up some tenure/accrued benefits, willingness to take some of the company's input in your sabbatical planning
- Willingness to recruit and train a replacement

Your proposal now makes clear the benefits the organization will achieve from your sabbatical, but what about the costs and what are you asking for in terms of support? It is unlikely that, unless your sabbatical policy provides for it, you will be able to take a sabbatical on full pay and benefits (take it if you can get it!), at least beyond a short period of time. Are you asking for half-pay beyond that, no pay but full benefits, or something in between? Do you want tuition support while on sabbatical? Finally, is the organization able to promise that you will get your old (or an equivalent) job back when you return?

7.7 Risk management

Finally, put together a risk-management plan. That means identifying the risks to your sabbatical's success, and determining what you plan to do for each of these to make sure they don't get in the way of your sabbatical. Understand that from an employer's perspective, they are taking a chance on your sabbatical. Some of these risks are:

- You may not return to work after your sabbatical. (Are you ready to make a commitment that you will, at least for a set period of time – even at the cost of retroactively losing some of your benefits or pay if you do not?)
- You may not be able to find and train a replacement in time for your sabbatical. (Are you ready to commit that you will only start your sabbatical when a replacement is in place and trained to your manager's satisfaction?)
- There is much more work coming up, and considering letting you go right now seems foolish. (Are you ready to delay your sabbatical until a critical project is complete? Are you ready to provide limited, remote support to your organization while on sabbatical?)
- The organization has never done anything like this before – it just "seems risky." (Offer to work with your organization's human resources and legal department in using your experience as a "pilot" to a sabbatical policy; always stay flexible.)
- If we grant your sabbatical request, everyone will want to go on sabbatical at once. (Remind your organization that it is up to them to define a sabbatical policy that makes sense for them, and that no sabbatical policy could allow anything that stops the business, but would rather "stagger" sabbatical requests and only grant these requests to high-value workers; also remind them that sabbaticals are an excellent way of retaining their best workers.)

7.8 Wrap-up: elements of a sabbatical proposal

A sabbatical proposal should have the following sections:

- Introduction and summary of request
- Summary background of yourself, brief history with the organization, key accomplishments, service on organization committees, working groups, and events, membership on job-related industry/professional groups, etc.
- Examples of your relationships with colleagues, clients, customers, patients, suppliers, and other business partners.
- Sabbatical goals – personal, and from the organization's perspective. Tie these in to the professional goals you have been discussing in past performance appraisals; in fact, your sabbatical request asks your organization to help you along towards achieving mutually defined goals.
- Value added to the organization from the sabbatical.
- Brief (one paragraph) description of proposed sabbatical activities, including proposed length and dates of sabbatical.
- Statement for how you will use the sabbatical to address areas for improvement as identified on past performance appraisals.
- Statement that you will display flexibility in your sabbatical goals and timing insofar as it still meets your overall personal goals for the sabbatical, and that you hope to mutually firm up these goals and timings with your management.

Present the proposal first as a draft, talk it through with decision makers, listen to their concerns and objections, alter the proposal as appropriate, and then present a final proposal for approval.

7.9 Negotiation

Negotiation can be one of the hardest crafts to master. Not once during my undergraduate business studies or graduate studies for a Masters of Business Administration (MBA) or law degree did I ever receive any formal training in negotiation. Let's face it – aside from those of us in customer interfacing sales roles, how many of us permanent employees ever had much negotiating to do anyway? After accepting an initial job offer, there is usually not much we negotiate over. And even then, how many of us leave the negotiations to a recruiter (who has their own interests and not ours at heart)?

Legions of books and courses teach the basics of negotiating, but most of what I learned was on the job, through trial and (a lot of) error. What I am about to express does not substitute for the depth that you can achieve through these resources; this is simply what I and others have found to be effective in sabbatical negotiations.

The first rule of negotiation is not to take the process personally. If it becomes clear through the negotiations that your negotiating partner is doing this, you have three choices: escalate to a negotiating partner higher in the organization, attempt to address the personal issues, or stop negotiating and move on. But we'll get to that.

Be prepared. You have your proposal in hand – but you are not yet ready. What you have to understand is your "bottom line." Your sabbatical plan and your proposal reflect what you want, and what you feel your employer needs, from your sabbatical. But the negotiating process may reveal other concerns you have not thought about, new information about upcoming business you could not have known about, or lines drawn in the sand that you did not anticipate. Expect surprises – and be prepared for them! Your employer may try to get you to back down on certain goals – how far will you bend before you break? Know how much you are willing to delay your sabbatical, or cut it short, or alter its goals, before it no longer appeals to you. Know up front how much contact with your organization you are willing to agree to while on sabbatical. And never tell your negotiating partner your bottom line, even if they ask for it – it is for you alone to know. If they find out, that will become their target – and they will start by offering you even less than this!

Make sure to establish and communicate your own credibility as an employee and as a negotiating partner. Know your strengths. Perhaps they are reliability, dependability, creativity, technical or mechanical skills, communication skills, knowledge of the organization, client contacts, contacts with other stakeholders, product knowledge, work process knowledge, experience with a proprietary system or process, leadership/team-building ability, customer service skills, or other. Reread copies of your old performance appraisals so that you can communicate how your strengths have been perceived by the organization.

Beyond credibility, ensure that you build and maintain trust throughout the negotiations. Say what you mean, and mean what you say. Do not promise one thing early on in the discussions to take it back later, and make sure that you are comfortable with and able to deliver on the commitments you do make.

Present your argument from a position of power. Are you "needed" by the organization? Are you involved in critical projects or initiatives that might suffer without you? Do you have critical and undocumented knowledge that you could offer to transfer in exchange for a sabbatical? Be ready to present your case strongly. Practice your presentation so that you do it with confidence.

Part of coming from a position of power is the financial and emotional security that comes with having a plan. Since you've already started thinking about going on sabbatical even without your employer's support, your confidence will shine through during the negotiations.

Next, you need to find out to whom you need to present your proposal. The best place to start is your organization's leave of absence or sabbatical policy, if it has one. Check your employee handbook as a starting point. If not, you should call your human resources representative and ask them how to present your proposal. Most likely, you should present it first to your manager but if not, ask how to keep your direct manager in the loop of your discussions. It is the nature of the working world that if your manager feels sidelined from the discussions they will be much more likely to resist a sabbatical in whatever ways they can. Share this concern with your HR department and hear what they have to say.

Now that you know who your negotiating partner is, you need to present your proposal. Unless there is a clear-cut policy for how to do this, endeavor to find out how your negotiating partner would prefer that this be done. They may not come right out and tell you this, so you will need to read the clues. What is their management style? Are they verbal, face-to-face type people or are they more comfortable with e-mail, reports, and the like? For the former, you should first present your proposal verbally, leave them with a copy of your written proposal, and ask to set a follow-up meeting (at their convenience) to discuss next steps. For the latter, it may be an idea to send them a written copy to peruse, and then set up a meeting to discuss it further. Ask those that are close to the negotiating partner how best to approach them with a proposal (but don't tell them what it is – you want to be the one to present it).

At some point, you will meet face-to-face with your negotiating partner to discuss your sabbatical. Start by educating them about what a sabbatical is. Many sabbatical books will tell you not to call your sabbatical a sabbatical, but a "leave of absence" or the like – this is nonsense. True, many in business and industry may look at sabbaticals as for academics only – fine! Make sure to let them know about all the research conducted by academics on sabbatical, the books written, the patents applied for, the technology developed, the ideas born, and the theories turned into practice. This is exciting stuff – make the most of it. Then launch into your proposal.

At any rate, during your first discussion, make sure to listen and take notes. It may be that your compelling proposal has already won them over, and they just want to wish you good luck. On the other extreme, they may tell you that a sabbatical is not possible. Most likely, the response you receive may be somewhere in between: agreement with the idea and value but too many concerns to consider moving forward.

Keep your chin up and do not take a first "no" as final – persistence, listening, flexibility, and a bit of cunning can help you win. Ask – why? Why not? What if…? What do you advise that I do? See if there is anything that you can give in order to turn the "no" into a "yes." Conversely, be careful not to accept their first offer unless it is close to your ideal situation. Try to gain more concessions to move closer to your idea.

If the replies you get to these probing questions are broad or sketchy, ask them to elaborate: "How exactly won't this work?" "If you say the company will not get benefit from my sabbatical, how could I restructure the sabbatical so it does?" And so on. Ask if the organization has any suggestions that would make this sabbatical more do-able. However, do not yet make counterproposals and do not quickly accept counteroffers. Do not get defensive, and do not counterattack. Learn the tricks of "dealing with difficult people." Listen to them; do not get drawn into arguing with them, get them to agree and accumulate "yeses," reframe questions, use open-ended questions, and so on.

As much as possible, establish rapport with them through listening and empathizing with their concerns and problems. Listen to their objections, concerns, and suggestions, promise to think about them, and to come back with a revised proposal. At the end of the meeting, summarize what you see their key points to be, thank them for their time, and ask to set up one more meeting.

There may come a time when it is apparent that your negotiating partner is not negotiating in good faith, and is openly hostile to you or your proposal. If they are the ultimate decision maker, then there may be little you can do. If not, you can escalate the negotiations to their management, or other senior managers of the organization.

If you're at the stage where they have considered your proposal and are offering counterproposals, go back and think about their position vis-à-vis (in relation to) your bottom-line negotiating position. Can you adapt your goals, timing, and strategy to address their concerns and suggestions without compromising your bottom line? For example:

- Would you take a voluntary layoff if your company is in financial difficulties (in exchange for a severance payment)?
- Would you be willing to trade time off for money (raise, bonus, or even take a salary cut)?
- Could you borrow from next year's vacation time, or can you combine earned sick, vacation, and personal days?
- Will you time your sabbatical to start during a slow period, if one exists for your profession/company (e.g., accountants, real-estate brokers, construction, tourism, etc.)?
- Can you agree on "take-backs" that can add value to the company when you return?
- Would you commit to staying for a certain period of time after your return (similarly to when an employer pays for education). In fact – make this argument – this is similar to paying for education!

If so, rewrite your proposal and prepare to present the revisions. When you do, start by thanking them for their comments and for the opportunity to re-present your sabbatical proposal. Next, outline the terms of your new proposal, making sure to emphasize the areas you have changed to meet their needs.

It is important to negotiate the argument and not get drawn into personalities. Try to channel some of Mr. Spock from Star Trek into your personality – keep cool, logical, and professional at all times. Even if the tone of the discussions becomes emotional, try to keep the discussion focused on problem solving. Never make the discussion a case of "us versus them," but of two parts of the same organization trying to solve a common business problem.

Win arguments through various tricks that experienced negotiators are familiar with. Use silence to draw your negotiating partner out. We are trained to think that every question or statement warrants a response – but a silent response can often create good "tension" on the part of your partner, and cause them to volunteer concessions or more information. Ask open-ended questions to draw out their position even further. Ask for clarification even if they are being very clear – it can also put an inexperienced negotiator on edge. Finally, actively invite criticism and advice. This allows you to determine their position and strategy so that you can win the argument.

Communicate that nearly everyone (perhaps even your negotiating partner?) may not want to do their job day in and day out until retirement – as much as they may love their job. That said, would your organization want to lose the experience and training that they have vested in you? Are you that easily replaceable? Don't they want to invest in their best people?

At a certain point however, the discussions will end – hopefully through agreement, but possibly with a firm "no" on the part of the organization. If you are confronted with the latter, you should know in advance how you will react. Are you prepared to tell them that it's you or your sabbatical – are you ready to quit on the spot? This is your ultimate bargaining tool but not one to use lightly or bluff with. If you are really prepared to go it alone though (you've been through the financial planning already, right?), this may be the last chance of getting a shot at an employee-sponsored sabbatical. But also be prepared for this not to end very nicely – you may be asked to leave quicker than you planned. So if your financial plan counts on a number of months more of income, perhaps you should just thank your negotiating partner for their time, and then walk away quietly.

Once an agreement has been reached, make sure to formalize and document it. Write down all of the terms, conditions, and agreements discussed – including any employment obligations, rights, and benefits you will retain during and after your sabbatical – and ask your management or human resources department to sign this document.

7.10 Drawbacks of company sponsorship

We should not close this discussion without mentioning some of the drawbacks of company sponsorship. First, such sponsorship rarely comes without strings attached (promises to stay with the organization after the sabbatical, obligation to work to some extent or stay in touch with the office while on sabbatical, time limits on the sabbatical, commitment to meet certain goals on sabbatical, etc.). You need to make sure you are comfortable with those strings. Moreover, company-sponsored programs are usually not available to temporary workers, contractors, or consultants (an increasingly significant part of the workforce). Finally, what you may need most is to make a break from your work environment, in order to rest and focus on personal growth. The temptation of a company safety net should not divert you if this is the case.

8: Self-Employed/Small Business Owners

Planning a sabbatical raises special challenges for the self-employed and those involved with a small business. Make no mistake though: these challenges can be met. In fact, there are advantages for the self-employed and small business owner:

- There is no line manager for you to convince
- You are already used to goal-setting, planning, managing tasks and people, and budgeting
- You are, most likely, already experienced in financial planning for downtime and "off periods" in your business
- Unlike an employee, it may be easier to take on more work ahead of a sabbatical to save more money
- You are already used to risk-management and contingency planning

But of course you will start asking the inevitable question – how can I leave my business alone? If you seriously care about your business, you should already be thinking about a succession plan. Think about it – if you cannot leave your business for a year or so, then how much depth do you have in its management? In fact, how many real vacations have you taken – especially without checking in to your office? Everyone likes to feel indispensable, but as the saying goes: "the graveyard is filled with indispensable people!" Small business owners who feel indispensable find it hard to let go, and have most likely created a business where every key decision comes from or gets approved by them.

If the business stops when you leave it for a little while, that is poor planning plain and simple. How are you really providing for your family's financial future, if something happens to you? Come on now – you can apply that creativity that made your business a success to coming up with a good succession plan. And you know that the time you spend on sabbatical can let you step back from your business, fight burnout, grow your creativity and perspective, and help you grow your business in new ways.

Management cross-training and succession planning is not just a very good idea – they are controls that banks and other credit providers increasingly look for before they extend credit. So if your small business has any aspirations of growing past a start-up stage into a mature and lasting enterprise, this is an issue you should address anyway. Planning a sabbatical is an excellent excuse to get a head start on this.

Who can you hire or train to back you up while on sabbatical? A family-operated small business may be in a good position for one of the family members to take a sabbatical (just be prepared to return the favor). Perhaps you are willing to arrange your business as a partnership. Either way, this role must be filled by someone you trust. This is also an excellent opportunity to groom the right family member for management duties.

One idea is to document your workflow, methods, and procedures. Prepare your backup on pending and new projects/business – but also make sure to tie up important loose ends yourself. Realize that you still may need to make yourself available while on sabbatical to deal with extraordinary or unexpected situations – but this should not be a regular occurrence. At any rate, it is important to inform your colleagues, clients, and other business partners of your sabbatical plans beforehand, letting them know who to contact in your absence and under which circumstances they should contact you. Set expectations as to how often you will (or will not) be checking in with them.

On the other hand, let's say that you are self-employed, running a one-man/one-woman show. You, like me, may be an independent contractor or freelancer. Here, you should be shooting for one or both of the following objectives: (a) doing something over your sabbatical to foster your professional growth, and (b) applying your skills in a working sabbatical. The first objective includes training and education, skills acquisition, market research, or other business development. The second option involves applying your current expertise to paid or volunteer work. Because many freelancers will not have guaranteed work or benefits when they return, I highly recommend a working sabbatical. Besides making the finances a bit easier, this will keep you "in the game" even when you've got one foot out of it, and will make it that much easier to transition back into a full working pattern after your sabbatical.

9: How to Plan

Reading some books about sabbaticals can be exciting, as we are taken along on the author's own experiences. The personal stories about years off in France studying painting, or a year traveling the world's adventure spots with the family, are fascinating and inspiring. At the same time it is difficult to glean from these books how exactly these sabbaticals were planned, as we struggle to find helpful information about how these sabbaticals were researched, organized, financed, discussed, argued about, and finally put together.

We should never think that planning a sabbatical is not a big affair. But by using a comprehensive methodology to approach planning, and by breaking things down into manageable tasks, the seemingly impossible can become reality.

Planning itself is a craft that can be taught and learned – it is not some innate ability that some have and others do not. Have you ever conducted research for school, a job, or a personal event? I'll bet that many of you have created a project plan for work, a financial plan, a career plan, a relocation plan, or some other sort of plan. Do you keep a "to do" list or a calendar?

A sabbatical plan is a combination of these activities. The plan is structured in such a way that it defines milestones, tasks, and activities and makes it clear the order in which all these tasks and activities need to happen. Another important aspect is that it makes it clear who takes which actions. But over all, the plan must make sense. We'll see how to make this happen.

9.1 Planning guidelines

First and foremost, you need to have set your goals and researched your sabbatical alternatives by now. A plan is simply a series of steps that needs to be timed and taken to make one of these sabbatical alternatives happen. The process of planning will help you choose amongst a few alternatives – and will also force you to have a backup plan in case one of these alternatives does not work out.

How much time do you need to plan? In a financial sense, the more time you have to save for your sabbatical, the better. You also need time to put together and execute a plan, meet deadlines, wait for decisions, negotiate, and make arrangements. A good rule of thumb is to start laying the groundwork at least a year before you go on sabbatical, longer if possible. You may need that much time to arrange things at work and plan for your time off. Many sabbatical options that require you to apply to a program (or find a working sabbatical opportunity) have application deadlines well in advance of the actual program start. Work visas can take several months to arrange. Don't wait until the last minute to make arrangements or you'll waste precious time off handling logistics.

Another planning trick is to start at the top, then "drill down." This means that you should not get hung up on details in the beginning of your planning. Instead, focus on a roadmap and on major planning milestones.

9.2 Milestones

First, from your goals and a few short-listed candidate sabbatical opportunities, express major milestones or transformations. These are those points that represent meaningful signposts in your plan. They help you to measure and rejoice in your progress along the way to your plan by telling you when something important has been accomplished.

At this stage, I suggest that you draw up a separate plan for each alternative – this is in fact excellent planning if any of these alternatives involves uncertainty (will your employer sponsor your sabbatical in some way, will you get that part-time job, will you get into that academic or study program, will you meet the necessary financial goal for that alternative, etc.). Typical milestones could be:

- Complete self-assessment
  o Determine current situation, finances, budget, family situation, other considerations
- Define goals, priorities, and success criteria
- Research, generate, prioritize, and cost alternatives
- Formulate initial sabbatical financial plan
- Implement sabbatical financing plan
- Finalize sabbatical proposal
- Apply to alternatives/submit sabbatical proposal
- Apply to children's schools
- Apply for visas
- Make decisions on proposals and applications

- Finalize sabbatical financial plan
  - o Determine sabbatical costs
  - o Determine funding sources
  - o Consult tax and financial-planning professionals
  - o Make insurance arrangements
- Formulate plans for sabbatical destination
  - o Arrange medical examination
  - o Book flights
  - o Arrange housing
  - o Arrange shipping
- Plan home decommissioning
  - o Rent/swap/keep home
  - o Cancel or transfer utilities, memberships, subscriptions
  - o Change address
- Formulate work transition plan
- Formulate contingency plan
- Formulate reentry/sabbatical exit plan
- Finalize overall sabbatical plan
- Reach financial goal
- Go on sabbatical
- Return from sabbatical

9.3 Timing

You then need to attach an approximate timeline to these milestones. Don't worry if these are not fully accurate yet – that will come once you more precisely define the tasks and sub-tasks that are associated with each milestone. At this stage, make sure to take into account any calendar deadlines for milestones like sabbatical alternative applications. For example, most universities and schools have application deadlines that cannot be missed. If you are submitting a proposal to your employer, there may or may not be firm deadlines there. Regardless, if you will be starting any sabbatical employment, study, or joining any other formalized program, there is likely to be a firm start date you need to take into account. Alternatively, if you are seeking an employer-sponsored sabbatical, are there any timing considerations that would dictate the choice of a start and end date? Does your job involve a busy season and a less busy season? When are critical projects starting, and ending?

Besides calendar deadlines, you should have an idea of how long your sabbatical financing plan will take to implement based on your estimate of sabbatical costs. Do you need one year to save/invest/work for the money you need for your sabbatical? Six months? Two years? You will have more precision in your dates once detailed tasks are described.

9.4 Deliverables

Deliverables are physical "things" created within your sabbatical project that let you track progress against milestones and goals. Your project plan itself is a deliverable, as are your goals and objectives statement, project risk-management plan, work visas, acceptance letters, contracts or agreements to take a paid/unpaid employer-sponsored sabbatical, leases, etc.

9.5 Drilling down to tasks and activities

Once your milestones are clear, you need to define all of the activities that make up that milestone. For example, let's explore the milestone "sabbatical proposal." What tasks make up this milestone? Typically, this will involve:

- Drafting a proposal
- Reviewing the proposal with family/friends/trusted peers
- Scheduling an appointment to present the proposal
- Presentation of the proposal
- Incorporation of feedback into the proposal
- Re-presenting a revised proposal
- Make decision to accept or reject

Doing this breakdown of tasks will have a few important benefits. First, you will ensure that you haven't forgotten anything. Next, you will have a better basis for estimating timings of milestones (and of your overall project plan). Finally, you will have a better idea of which tasks and milestones depend on others – so you can better manage your plan.

9.6 Dependencies

Dependencies are linkages between the tasks, milestones, and deliverables of a project. They arise because of what is feasible, and because of resource constraints. They are important to identify so you can properly sequence and time the various tasks in your plan. If one task depends on an earlier task completing, and that earlier task in turn depends upon others, it is easier to figure out how long a sequence of tasks will take and also easier to know which tasks, if delayed, can delay your entire plan.

One type of dependency is where a certain task can only start once another one has finished. For example, certain countries will only let you apply for a work visa if you already have a job offer; in this case, the "job offer letter" deliverable must be in place before the "apply for visa" task starts. Another type of dependency is where one task or milestone cannot finish until another one finishes. You cannot finalize your sabbatical financial plan until you have a decision on which sabbatical alternative you will pursue.

Make sure to track what project planners call "external dependencies" – other things in your life not necessarily part of your sabbatical plan that may affect your sabbatical plan (whether they be day-to-day events, less frequent periodic events, or one-off happenings). If you are suddenly offered a promotion or a transfer at work, and if this affects your sabbatical plan or timing, you know you have an external dependency you need to watch out for.

How do you discover dependencies? It's really very easy. After defining your milestones, deliverables, and tasks, ask yourself the following for each task: Can I start this task right now? If the answer is no, ask why not? Typically, that task needs another task to be completed first; that task, in turn, may depend upon one or more others. For example, a task "apply for an educational visa" can only be completed once the task "provide an official university acceptance letter" has been completed. And the latter may only be completed once the "apply to university task" and "get accepted to university" milestones have passed.

Sophisticated project management software (including Microsoft Project) can track dependencies, and take them into account when estimating project time, cost, and resourcing (see Figure 9.6.1 Project Plan Calendar). If you are familiar with and have access to these tools, they can help you enormously. Otherwise, you can maintain your plan in a simple spreadsheet and you can track dependencies within the spreadsheet. The flow chart showing the different stages of this planning process is also a useful tool (see Figure 9.6.2 Project Plan Flow Chart).

Figure 9.6.1 Project Plan Calendar

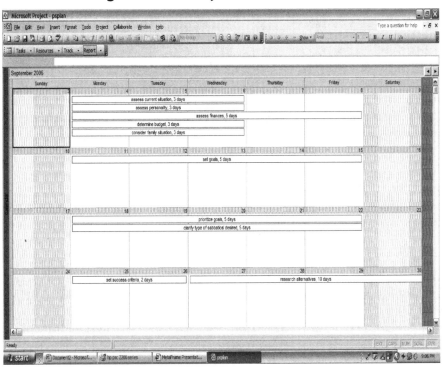

Microsoft Project can help you create a calendar with tasks assigned to the appropriate days if you use this software to create a project plan.

Figure 9.6.2 Project Plan Flow Chart

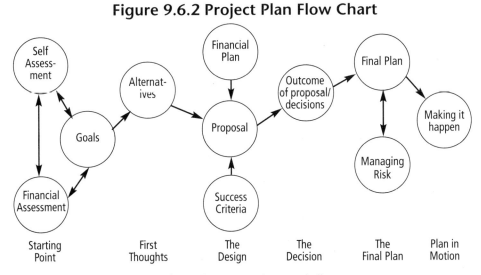

The project process in a nutshell.

9.7 Task estimation and assigning resources

How long do you plan to stay on sabbatical? To an extent, it depends on many things:

- How long you have agreed to stay on sabbatical (if you are being sponsored)
- How long your sabbatical program will last (if you are enrolling in a formal program of study, volunteering, or work commitment)
- How long you want/need to stay, based on personal considerations and so on.
- How much you can afford (if you are not being sponsored)

As a general rule, the longer the sabbatical, the more people coming on sabbatical with you, the more people depending on you back home, or the more complicated your sabbatical goals, the more complex a plan you will have. If you are single, have few dependents, and are planning a shorter sabbatical in a single location, you can get by with less involved up-front planning than a family planning on traveling the world for a year.

For each task, you should estimate how long you expect it to take. For tasks that you have done before, this should be straightforward. If there were similar tasks that you had accomplished, you can use the estimates for those tasks. Otherwise, you will need to "guesstimate" the task length based on your research, the information you gather from others who have done something similar, or even plain intuition. When in doubt, leave extra time in the task estimation to manage this uncertainty.

Since this is your sabbatical plan, it is likely that you will be doing most of the work in making it happen. However, there may be tasks that you "assign" to others (family, friends, etc.) and there may be tasks that others must perform (a consulate, your employer, a bank, etc.). Make sure to track "who does what" in your plan so you can hold people (including yourself) to it!

9.8 The to-do list and calendar – making it happen

Nowadays, many of us have electronic to-do lists and calendars in our phones, personal digital assistants (PDAs), and computers. A paper-based version will do just as well. The idea is to put your upcoming tasks into your to-do list for easy tracking and reminders. You can track your overall milestones and your important deliverables (acceptance letter, application deadlines, etc.) in your calendar. The goal is to make it as easy as possible to keep to your plan.

For example, when we were applying for our travel visas we were told we needed an "apostille" on key documents (all of our birth certificates and our marriage certificate). This turned out to be a mini-project unto itself – here is how we tracked this in our mobile phone's to-do list (see Figure 9.8 To-Do List for Apostilles).

Figure 9.8 To-Do List for Apostilles

- Obtain "long form" birth certificates
- Obtain letter of certification for each birth certificate
- Obtain "long form" marriage license
- Bring birth certificates and certifications to the state offices for original signatures
- Bring marriage certificate to the city offices for original signatures
- Bring birth certificates and marriage certificate to the state notary office for verification of signature
- Bring notarized birth certificates to the offices of the Department of State for official apostille

---

9.9 Risks and contingency planning

Identify risks to your project's success – risks you won't meet project goals and objectives, risks of not meeting key timelines. Think "what if," and "what will this mean." For example:

- What if the task is not performed correctly?
- What if I need help doing certain tasks?
- What if the task is delayed, or was incorrectly estimated?
- What if there are new tasks, that I never thought of, that need doing?
- What if there are dependencies between tasks, or lead times before certain tasks can begin, that I didn't think of?

Then think about what you can do in these or other likely scenarios:

- Are there more tasks that you need to add to your plan?
- Are you applying to alternatives (as with "second choice" colleges)?
- Are you unable to raise the required money for your sabbatical? Have you raised enough to borrow the rest on credit?
- Can you accept alternatives if the deliverables or decisions planned for are not attained (acceptance decision, sponsorship, choice of destination, choice of accommodations, etc.)?
- Can you get help doing certain tasks?
- Do you need to allow more time for other tasks – or recognize dependencies?
- Is your visa application interminably delayed? Do you have alternate destinations in mind?

Start by revising your project plan with any new information (date changes, dependencies, extra tasks, additional resources, or even changed deliverables). Then make sure this new plan is something you can live with (but have more confidence that your revised plan is much more accurate and do-able, something that can make your sabbatical work).

As with risk management, contingency planning is a mind-set and a set of skills required of any good project planner – you need to acquire these yourself. Define a contingency plan by asking what if the sabbatical isn't working out or you run out of money? What if events begin to compel you to return? You cannot think through every scenario but at least think through the realistic and likely ones, and come up with some well thought-out responses:

- Adjust your goals
- Cut sabbatical expenses (housing, overall location)
- Cut the sabbatical short
- Obtain more financing

9.10 Take a step back

Let a few days pass after writing down your plan. Then take a critical look at what you've done:

- Are the decision points and risks clear?
- Are the milestones, tasks, and deliverables clear and understandable?

- Are the tasks described in enough detail so that you know what exactly needs to be done – or do you need to drill down further?
- Did you leave time for the unexpected – and for simple relaxation?
- Have you kept expectations, goals, and timings realistic?
- Have you left enough time for yourself in your plan – or have you over-scheduled your sabbatical?
- Is it clear what depends upon what, and who needs to do what to make this plan happen?

If something looks like it does not make sense, it probably does not. Wherever you are estimating ("guesstimating") how long something takes or what exactly is involved, ask someone more knowledgeable about that topic for their opinion.

9.11 Check your assumptions

At this stage, your goals are clear, you are assessing alternatives, and you now have drafted a plan. Now you need to check your assumptions (whether implicit or explicit in your plan). Consider the following:

- Are you banking on certain tax write offs, refunds, or other breaks in your sabbatical financial plan?
- Do your care arrangements for your aging mother depend upon your sister's cooperation or upon your mother's willingness to assign decision-making powers to your or your sister?
- Does your sabbatical financing plan hinge upon your obtaining part-time work while on sabbatical (a working sabbatical)? When will you know whether this can be done?
- Are there other ways to finance your sabbatical if you cannot find work?
- Are you assuming that you will be in good enough health to take the type of sabbatical you want to take?

Now is the time to start checking these assumptions. If you are counting on someone else to do something, explain why this is and ask them for their commitment. If you are counting on an event to happen (get a job, get employee sponsorship, collect a legal settlement, etc.), understand the probability that this event will occur – and have a backup scenario if it does not. If you need confirmation from an expert (lawyer, accountant, tax professional, doctor, etc.) whether something is feasible, check with them.

9.12 Track progress

Determine how you will track progress against your plan. For each task/milestone/deliverable, you should assign a unique activity number, start date, end date (or duration), dependency if applicable, assigned resource name, and percentage completion. In the beginning, you may want to review your plan every couple of weeks to track progress and note any changes to the plan. As you get more advanced in executing your plan, you may want to do this every week. If you find that your plan is always changing, or if you are varying significantly from your time estimates, make sure to double check that your vision and sabbatical goals will still be met. Then go back and have a second look at your plan – it may be unrealistic.

9.13 The forced sabbatical

If you've been laid off and want to make the most of your forced sabbatical, take heart and follow the same steps we've been discussing. As much as you are likely to focus your thoughts on why you were fired and what you think you could have done to avoid it, try to think instead about what your career and life needs now. In this vein, you still need to assess your situation, develop goals, and come up with a plan the same way as any other sabbatical-taker. You will simply be eliminating certain steps and curtailing others; for example:

- You will not be planning to save for your sabbatical for a year or more, since it's started already! The goal here is to assess your finances (hopefully you have a severance or separation payment to supplement your savings), and determine what you can do with what you have. Certainly a working sabbatical deserves serious consideration.
- You may want to identify and avoid alternatives that have long lead times, like getting accepted into an academic or continuing-education program, unless this is one of your primary sabbatical goals. Almost certainly, you will want to eschew taking a sabbatical in a country with long visa application times if there are others that make the process quicker and easier.
- Making a sabbatical proposal to an employer obviously doesn't make much sense anymore.

10: Handling Objections

10.1 Expect objections

It's inevitable. Even after you've planned and psyched yourself, others around you will still doubt. You will hear from family, friends, colleagues, managers, clients, and others. Some will support you, some will be unsure, and others will openly voice disapproval. You must learn to expect objections. But which ones are valid and worth listening to, and which are at best "noise" and at worst demotivating?

You should realize by now that the very suggestion of a sabbatical is foreign to most people. Your idea may sound new and strange, and it may take a bit of educating before the objector gets used to it. Initial objections sometimes change into support after more careful thought. Start by understanding the motivations behind objections. It could be that they originate out of concern for you. On the other hand, they may reflect the self-interest of the objector, or some desire to compete with or even harm you. Do the objections stem from ignorance, or jealousy? Perhaps the objector is being judgmental. Think about where they are coming from and why they may be objecting – a source with good intentions should always be heeded more than one without.

Also, you must factor in who is voicing the objection. Is it a partner or immediate family member? Perhaps it is a close friend, or other family or friends. On the other hand, it may be a boss, co-worker, or casual acquaintance. Plainly, some people matter more than others to you. The views of those you trust should be heard.

In the end, how you handle and respond to these objections depends upon these factors. Your options are to:

- Listen
- Involve the objectors in your project planning
- Adapt your plans
- Argue/convince the objector
- Ignore the objections

10.2 Types of objections

By this point, many of the "common" objections should be themes you have already thought about and factored into your plans. These include objections based upon:

- Circumstances (in effect, concerns about finances, health care/insurance coverage, career, family, self-worth tied to job, losing skills, not keeping up within an organization, maintaining a small business, losing clients/business, not providing support to family and friends, and so on)
- "Morality" (the Protestant work ethic, indulging in "the rich man's whimsy" especially if you are well-off)
- Personality ("you are not the type to do this," "with your history, do you really think you can make this work")
- Timing (not the right time, taking a sabbatical in an environment of downsizing, bad economy, or outsourcing of jobs)

If you've done your self-assessment and sabbatical planning (including your financial planning) you should have no problem countering these objections with the facts.

10.3 Those close to you

A partner's initial objection to a sabbatical is not a tragedy – it is an opportunity. Many married couples don't communicate well about planning for the future – whether for children's education, retirement, or other financial goals. Ponder how much you really know about your partner's financial and other priorities, and they about yours. Grab this perfect opportunity to begin a dialogue. After all, a sabbatical is also an opportunity to turn the normal dynamics of a marriage or relationship on its head. If one spouse normally has more "power" than the other (typically the one who earns more money), a sabbatical can put both partners on equal footing and restore a healthy balance to the relationship.

Parents' reactions may not be any easier. They may feel betrayed and abandoned particularly if you have children, and may not at all understand what you want to do and why. You may crave their support but get none. You need to draw upon the wellsprings of your inner strength when external approval and support is not forthcoming.

All in all, you should do your best to depersonalize comments as much as possible (admittedly easier said then done when the comments come from family and loved ones), remove the emotion, and listen to the real arguments underneath.

10.4 Worthwhile objections

So you've discovered some important questions to which you do not have answers. Do you throw in the towel and forget about a sabbatical? Do you just ignore these questions? Hopefully not, but it depends upon whether the objection is something which can be addressed by adjusting your plan or your timing in such a way that it does not compromise your core sabbatical goals.

Let's look at some examples of this. You are saving enough to comfortably take a sabbatical. Your goals are clear, and you have a good plan. You feel confident that you will return from the sabbatical refreshed, and with new skills that will help you in your career. But there's a catch. If you leave now, you will forgo a guaranteed bonus in nine months. Do you stay and collect the bonus, and take your sabbatical afterwards? If the bonus is enough to change your circumstances, it may be worth waiting for. On the other hand, if you were accepted in a certain academic or research program that you planned to pursue during your sabbatical, delaying the start of your sabbatical may not be feasible or desirable.

Let's mix this up a bit. Instead of a bonus, you are up for a key promotion. Is now the right time to go on sabbatical? It depends. How "ready" are you for the sabbatical (meaning, can you last until you receive this promotion)? Evaluate how important the promotion would be for your career – and for your life. Once you receive this promotion, would you be less likely to take a sabbatical?

In nearly all cases, the issue is when to take a sabbatical rather than if. Promotions, the birth of a child, an anticipated bonus, or other milestones may be worth waiting for first, but all that means is postponing your sabbatical for a while. You simply need to be careful where events you are anticipating may or may not happen. Nowadays, fewer but a not insignificant number of workers tend to think that their company will "take care of them," causing them to dismiss the idea of a sabbatical as an act of disloyalty. Maybe they will, maybe they won't, but you know that you can take care of yourself best, right?

If you do make the decision to postpone a sabbatical, keep plugging on with a sabbatical plan and start executing a sabbatical savings plan now – you will have that much more money when you are ready and that many more alternatives open to you. In other cases, the solution amounts to scheduling your sabbatical during a natural transition in your life, such as a job change, house move, relocation, long vacation, job loss, pregnancy leave, inheritance/settlement/payout, and so on.

10.5 Questioning your responsibility

You are likely to have your sanity called into question from across the spectrum – family, friends, co-workers, associates, etc. This is one of the least substantial objections there is, since it originates from a conformist viewpoint that would suggest "most people don't take sabbaticals, so therefore those that do must be crazy." Don't compare your path and plans with those of others. And remember that your plan is not "irrational" if it is in fact a well thought-out plan that considers your goals and circumstances.

We have already discussed the need to be responsible to your self as well as to others. Like so many aspects of life, the answer to this objection lies in moderation and not the extremes. A power sabbatical is indeed of primary benefit to the sabbatical-taker, but that does not make it a narcissistic experience, since it involves growth as well as rest. It is no more a crime to take care of these needs than it is to get enough sleep, eat right, and exercise.

"Taking children out of their school and environment and routine will be bad for them." I find this to be one of the more foolish objections, unless your child has special needs that simply cannot be met in your sabbatical destination (even then, perhaps an alternate destination could be considered). Will a sabbatical not enrich them? We took our daughter with us on many business trips, a summer in Amsterdam, and on extended stays in London and in Israel, where she attended school. As a result, she is exponentially more worldly and knowledgeable about other cultures and places than other children, even in cosmopolitan New York City. When her teachers ask her class about Van Gogh, she can honestly say she's seen many of his best works in Amsterdam. Isn't that the best education you can get? If you suspect that taking a child out of their current routine will have deleterious effects, consult with their educators, a doctor, or a child psychologist first.

It is important for children to take along some familiar and beloved objects and possessions with them. Yet as long as children are with their parents on sabbatical, they will usually surprise you with how well they adapt. If relatives and close friends can visit during the sabbatical, then that would be a treat for them to look forward to and something to remind them of home. It is also important for them to know that a sabbatical is not forever, particularly if they are young and cannot understand the concept of time. At any rate, you should have a good idea of how much attention your children need; this will determine whether/how you can work while on sabbatical, what type of day-care or schooling options to consider (home schooling versus tutoring versus international education versus local schooling). And needless to say, you should apply the same commonsense rules to child safety that you would apply at home – and even more so in an unfamiliar environment.

10.6 Co-workers

With the exception of those whose opinions you really trust, don't take the complaints of co-workers too seriously. People talk – and people in offices talk a lot! Objections, disapproval, and scorn are to be expected from many in the workplace since in many cases these feelings originate from jealousy, envy, and fear about losing a valuable colleague if only for a while. It should not be surprising that most co-workers are stuck with their in-the-box thinking – after all, what are they doing about their own situations and challenges? Thinking about it, you would probably feel the same in their shoes. For your part, do not gloat over your sabbatical – keep a low profile. Do not respond to every objection, just ones that are patently untrue that could damage your standing in your organization. And in the end – you wouldn't mind proving the doubters wrong, would you?

10.7 The unknown

How do you know what lies ahead when you leave the "safety" of your life here? How do you know what will be in store for you when you get back? This is a common refrain you will hear from family, friends, and co-workers alike. You already know that your project plan breaks the unknown down into manageable phases, tasks, deliverables, and milestones. You should also have confidence in your own abilities. Tell people about your plans, and it will create encouragement and positive pressure (by making it harder for you to back out!). And in terms of personal safety, you will display the same cautiousness and common sense to decisions like finding a place to live, locating a school, doing daily chores, and going out at night, such as you would apply at home.

We cannot discuss the unknown without mentioning its cousin – fear. Learn to separate fears based on (apparent) facts, and those based upon speculation. You will see that having the right mind-set, knowing why, having a plan, and a good proposal will help you conquer your fear of the unknown. For fact-based fears, consider whether any mitigating factors and circumstances make these facts less persuasive. Are these fact-based fears simply risks that you don't have a plan to manage? Then get to work and think about how you should manage them.

10.8 Support systems

In fairness, a sabbatical can be successful without a support network of friends, family, and an employer. Sometimes one must truly go it alone to find one's own way – even where it means bucking the disapproval of those you care about or doing without needed logistical help. But just as having more money can make a sabbatical easier on the wallet, having a support system can make it easier on the heart, mind, and body.

The object is not necessarily to "win over" all of your friends, family, and colleagues. Rather, you first want someone who knows you well and will be honest with you to go over your plan and give you their thoughts. Maybe you've missed something. It could be that you are not being honest with yourself about your true financial situation, responsibilities, capabilities, personality, and so on. Your parents, siblings, other close relatives, and dear friends should be ready to be honest where you are not. It could be that you haven't studied your target sabbatical opportunity or location well enough. Perhaps you are not seeing certain risks in your plan that others do. Or maybe there is something that you don't yet know about that those close to you will now tell you (you have an inheritance, secret trust find, or other unforeseen source of money – or someone close to you is very sick and they haven't told you yet).

Yet listening to concerns and objections should rarely stop you from going on sabbatical. Instead, you will learn to filter out the emotions, personalities, and histories bound up with those close to you – and focus on the meat of their arguments. A true argument should have one of three results:

- You alter your sabbatical plan (self-assessment, goals, tactics, choice of alternative, financial plan) by making you consider things you missed
- You re-time your sabbatical
- You drop a sabbatical plan entirely for the near future

Parents and close relatives, for example, tend to blow hot or cold on a sabbatical depending upon several factors. If the sabbatical will bring you closer to them (perhaps you live far away and want to take a sabbatical closer to them), they are likely to show some measure of support. And the opposite is usually true as well – particularly if you are involved in caring for them. Parents will naturally display the usual concerns:

- How will you support yourself?
- Why are you uprooting yourself and your family?
- Where are you taking my grandkids?
- Is it safe where you're going?

So it pays to have some idea of your sabbatical plan before discussing this with them for the first time. But some parents may identify with the desire for rest and change, or for other reasons (wanting the best for you) will support your idea.

Generally friends will be more supportive than parents since they usually don't have the same stake in their relationship with you (though they care about you). Friends who want you to be happy and fulfilled, but don't rely on you for emotional, physical, or day-to-day support will by nature have less to object to. But you should listen to their concerns and arguments nonetheless. Remember too that your close friends will probably know things about you that even your parents do not – some of which may be relevant to your sabbatical plan.

Your immediate family (spouse, partner, children) are another story. Dig beyond any initial resistance to discover the root cause of these objections. Remember that concerns can range from the superficial, to worries about location, to lifestyle, to schools and friends, to health care, to simply not wanting to go on sabbatical at all. If you are dealing with the latter, you will have some serious thinking to do before going on sabbatical.

Their feelings about the sabbatical can run the gamut, depending on many things:

- Are they happy?
- Are they ready for a break or a change?
- Do they see mostly risks – or opportunities?
- Do they see where a sabbatical can benefit them as well as you?
- Where are they in their lives now?

With them, you must listen and with each immediate family member's input, you should decide whether a sabbatical is right and if so, whether the timing is right. Bur first, make sure to take all the time you need with them to explain why you need a sabbatical, and what options are open to them. Giving them some say in the sabbatical plan or the timing can go a long way to making it acceptable to them.

These discussions could result in modifications to your sabbatical plan and timings, particularly with regards to issues like child care, elder care, education plans, health-care arrangements, choice of destination and living arrangements, and the financial plan. Realize that there is an inevitable balancing act between satisfying the wants and needs of your immediate family and key support people, and meeting your sabbatical goals. On the other hand, you may want to call upon your support network to help you out during the sabbatical with day-to-day issues back home (whether as trivial as picking up mail, or as critical as providing temporary care to an elder in your care). Everyone's situation, support network, and sabbatical plan will be unique – so there is no single answer here other than to discuss, listen, analyze, and revisit plans where you need to.

11: Practical Arrangements

11.1 Managing your finances while away

There are two considerations in managing your finances while on sabbatical that become relevant if you are taking your sabbatical outside of your normal home: will you be within your home country, or will you be taking a sabbatical abroad? If you will be within your home country, then banking should be simpler (you will not need to worry about international banking issues like opening bank accounts in other countries, wire transfers, currency conversion, and so on). If you already have a banking relationship with a nation-wide bank with branches and ATMs in many locations, you probably do not need to do anything special. If you bank with a smaller local bank, then you may have some concerns: Will you be able to access cash at ATMs in other parts of the country if your bank does not participate in the relevant payments networks (ask your bank)? How will you be able to deposit money if they do not have a branch where you need it? Now may be the time to consider opening an account at a larger bank.

If you are going out of the country, it is more complex. Will you need a bank account, or can your current bank handle your banking requirements through a local branch in that country? If you need to open a local bank account (always helpful if you will be working), make sure you understand the requirements for doing so. Check first with your current bank – they may be able to help you open an account with a subsidiary or branch abroad. Or, you may need a letter of introduction and other references and documents to open a local account.

Better banking and credit-card services have made international banking much easier but if you will be in a country that does not have reliable or accessible bank machines you need a head start. In any case, purchase some local currency and traveler's checks in advance to get you started when you arrive. Make sure your credit cards are up-to-date or, if they will expire while you are away, arrange to have the new cards sent on to you. Make arrangements, such as automatic deductions, for paying bills and managing your cash. Most utilities and service providers offer electronic billing so that you can pay bills entirely online.

If your bank does not let you manage your money online, you should consider opening an account somewhere that does. If you plan to continue to receive bills and credit-card statements and the mail is slow, be prepared to pay interest and late charges.

Where opening a local account is a headache, there are alternatives. First, you can carry in local currency and traveler's checks from your own location. (Check local rules about how much currency can be brought in without further reporting requirements). Those countries' embassies, consulates, or official Web sites should point you in the right direction for finding out these rules. Of course, you don't want to carry too much cash for safety reasons; large denomination traveler's checks are a better bet. Another alternative is to draw cash from your credit or charge card. Visa and MasterCard allow you to do this in other countries, but American Express only allows you to draw this in their traveler's checks. Still another option is to wire money from your home bank to a bank in your sabbatical location (but you may already need a bank account at that location); an alternative is to use Western Union to wire money.

Leave some blank, signed checks and/or deposit slips in the hands of a trusted family member or friend for any unforeseen financial matters that may arise in your absence. Make sure you store cash, valuables, or negotiable instruments like stocks, bonds, and collectibles in a safety deposit box or bank vault before you leave. Finally, be sure to extend any licenses, registrations, or credit cards that would expire while you're away. You don't want your key credit card getting denied while on sabbatical (it almost happened to me)!

11.2 Taxes

You need to know two things. First, if you will be spending part of your sabbatical outside of the country, will you have to pay and file income taxes in that location? If so, under what circumstances would this occur? Consult a tax advisor familiar with your target country's tax laws. And if you are a U.S. taxpayer, you have the singular honor of having to pay your taxes every April 15th no matter where in the world you are living and working. Again, a qualified tax advisor is a necessity, since your tax situation when you are working and paying taxes abroad becomes much more complex.

Regardless of your nationality, if you will be working while abroad you should discuss the following with your tax advisor:

- How must taxes be paid?
- Where will your "domicile" be – according to your home and host countries?
- Where will your income originate?
- Which expenses and other items would be deductible?
- Will you have a home country tax liability?
- Will you have a local tax liability?
- Will you be able to offset the local against your home country tax liability?

11.3 What to do with your home

Whether you decide to rent your home while on sabbatical depends on several things. First, do you currently rent or own? If you rent, and if you go on sabbatical towards the end of your lease, perhaps it is easier to simply give up your apartment and find another one when you return, versus subletting it. If you own, the decision to rent can hinge on many things:

- Do you plan on coming back and forth during your sabbatical, and will you need a place to stay?
- Can you afford not to rent it out?
- If you rent it, would you have to store your personal effects? How much would that cost? What other costs associated with renting it would you need to bear?
- How long do you plan to be away? Many tenants may be less willing to accept a lease for less than one year, though this varies by location.

When we went on sabbatical, the terms of my own working sabbatical were to work a certain number of days per month in my old consulting contract at my old location, for the first few months of my sabbatical. I flew back and forth to Israel once a month to do this. We decided that it paid not to rent our house, so that I had somewhere to stay while doing this.

Don't overlook another excellent opportunity – a home swap. Using this system, you swap homes with someone in your target destination for a period of time ideally corresponding with that of your sabbatical. You avoid the need to find a tenant, and do not have to pay for housing in your destination (though you continue paying as you would in your home location). Unlike other tenants, house-swap partners are much more likely to take better care of your home since they know that you are living in theirs! The appendix has a list of the most established home-swap resources.

In any case, whether you are planning to rent or swap your home, begin making arrangements three to six months in advance.

11.4 Home maintenance

Whether you will rent your home or keep it vacant (but not of course if you sell or terminate your lease), you should make a list of things that need to be done to maintain your home. These include regular tasks and seasonal tasks. Think about things like:

- Canceling or suspending newspaper and magazine delivery
- Checking after storms or snow for downed trees, flooding, and other weather-related damage
- Cleaning gutters
- Disconnecting or suspending telephone and cable services
- Handling bills
- Keeping the house clean
- Keeping the house heated during winter
- Maintaining a pool
- Maintaining in-ground sprinkler pipes
- Maintaining lawn and garden
- Making someone available on the spot in an emergency
- Making sure owner's manuals or other instructions for operating utilities and appliances are available
- Organizing other annual mechanical maintenance
- Placing valuables in secure storage, or a safe deposit box or with relatives
- Reading utility meters and checking bill balances before you leave
- Receiving mail
- Removing snow
- Running water in the pipes
- Securing your home
- Storing your cars safely (get the advice of an auto mechanic)
- Ventilating the house in the summer
- Watching for mold

Draw up a limited power of attorney for a trusted relative or friend who is authorized to pay emergency bills (remember, you should endeavor to pay regular bills online or automatically). Leave them with a dedicated checking account to use.

Check with your homeowner's insurance agent, the company that monitors your home security system and your local police as to the best way to insure the safety of your property. This ought to be done even if you are subletting your home to others.

Finally, you confront the question of what to do with all of your stuff. Look at this as an excellent opportunity to do some intensive spring-cleaning – throw out things that are useless and not sellable, and sell or donate to charity those that are that you no longer need. (The latter will provide a sizable tax benefit in many countries). You can leave certain things in place in your home and rent it out furnished. Finally, you can store other items that are meaningful and which you do not want your tenants having access to. You can sell your car, donate it, rent it, store it, or keep it in a friend or relative's garage. If you are garaging or storing it, make sure to have a trusted individual start it and run it periodically, and take it for inspection.

11.5 How much?

How much can you rent your home for? The first and most important consideration is what the market will bear – in effect, what comparable homes rent for. A local, licensed real-estate broker should be able to help you find out. But will this be enough? In order to calculate an appropriate monthly rent, total your costs for mortgage payments, taxes, additional homeowner's insurance, cost of drawing up a lease, realtor's and management fees, and any utilities (cable TV, water, etc.) you will continue to pay, to determine the minimum rent you will need to charge so as not lose money on the rental. Compare this minimum estimate with market rents for your area to arrive at a reasonable figure for your home and your situation.

11.6 Check out potential tenants

The single best thing you can do to avoid problems later is to check tenants out up front. This means doing a full credit check and checking work and past landlord references. If possible, you should also do a criminal background check on your tenants. They should fill out a formal application form (available with a good landlord's reference book) and all information on the form should be verified.

Next, your potential tenants should be able to afford the rent. They should have regular, verifiable monthly gross income in the neighborhood of three to four times the rent amount and some degree of liquid assets (at least one year's worth of rent), in bank accounts or other accessible form. They should be able to put down a reasonable security deposit or certain number of months rent up front.

Finally, you can exercise some personal discretion. If no one in your home smokes, you may not want smokers renting your house during your sabbatical. Likewise, you may also want to think twice about renting to tenants with pets or small children if you don't have any of your own, or if you have especially delicate furniture and furnishings (then again, you could always store them away to keep them safe).

11.7 Draw up a lease

Whether you know your new tenants or not, draw up a lease with the help of a real-estate attorney (in many countries, the legal fee is tax deductible from your rental income). You can include anything in a lease that is legal and agreeable between the two parties. If possible, arrange for someone you trust in your area to make periodic visits to check on the state of the property (this would need to be agreed up front and drawn into the lease). That individual should meet the tenants before you leave. If you can have this person sign a "limited power of attorney" form, they can also help enforce the terms of the lease and act on your behalf should major repairs or legal actions be required.

The lease should spell out responsibility for maintaining the property during the rental period. Who is responsible for snow removal, lawn maintenance, leader and gutter cleaning, and other upkeep? Who is responsible for paying property tax and utility bills? If tenants will be responsible for utilities, make sure to change the billing to their name, so that the utilities will have no claim on you if they do not pay. Generally, if you want these things done to your standards, it is advisable to contract for a service to perform these functions – but how this would be reimbursed should be discussed and agreed in the lease.

Chances are you as landlord will be responsible for repairs – but what if they result from the tenant breaking something? And to what extent will you permit your tenant to remodel your home? (Painting or moving furniture may be allowable, but other permanent changes should normally not be.) This is where a good real-estate attorney can be invaluable.

11.8 Rental payments

If your bank offers this service, you can have your tenant send your rent checks directly to your bank. Most banks will also take post-dated rental checks and cash them on the first of the month. Alternatively, they can send the check to the individual who will be "standing in for you," or to some other trusted individual who can deposit these checks for you. Finally, you can have these sent to a management agent if you will be having one manage your property in your absence.

11.9 Household insurance

Check in with your insurance agent or homeowner's insurance company before you leave. If you are renting your home, you may require additional coverage. Some insurance companies will not insure your household effects while you rent, so you may have to shop around – or store these effects elsewhere, or else they will become the responsibility of your tenants.

11.10 Take a picture

Photograph the rooms and the property in your home right before you turn it over to tenants. Take close-ups of any detail. It is advisable to use a high-quality digital camera with a time and date stamp, in case these photos are needed later for an insurance claim or legal action. It is also a good idea to photograph the valuables that you will be taking with you, to move along any insurance claims later on.

Be careful about leaving your "stuff" around in their normal places. These can easily get mixed up with the tenant's property over the course of the lease period and may be moved with other items when the lease expires. Unless by specific agreement of the lease, you should consider moving all of your things to a separate room, preferably one that is off-limits to the tenant that you can lock up. Alternatively, you can move these to an off-site storage location.

11.11 Storage

If you are renting your home and need to store your personal items – and mom's basement just isn't big enough, you need to look into storage options. You can rent a monthly storage space (some even help you haul your things there). There are even door-to-door storage companies that drop off large storage crates at your home, which you pack and lock using your own locks. They then pick these up and store them for you.

I've used many types of storage methods over the years, and have the following recommendations:

- If you are storing anything of any importance, make sure the storage facility has its own security. It should be attended while the facility is open, and patrolled or covered by an alarm system when closed.
- The storage facility should be climate-controlled and have fire and flood alarms, and a sprinkler system.
- Ask about procedures to access your stored effects. They should insist on visitor identification first.
- Make sure they offer stored-goods insurance, and take advantage of it.
- Make sure they can set up regular credit-card billing or some other form of payment that is easy for you to handle while away on sabbatical.

11.12 Automobile storage and insurance

If you are leasing your vehicle, can you time your sabbatical around the end of the lease? If you own, is this a good time to sell your vehicle – or donate it to charity (which often yields a valuable tax deduction)? If not, and if you plan to leave your automobile at home while away, you will need to arrange for it to be stored safely. Check with your locality's policy and motor vehicle registration body for rules, regulations, and registration information. If you will not be driving your vehicle on sabbatical, check whether you can cancel your automobile insurance, or obtain information on how to add a new driver to your insurance policy and vehicle registration if someone else will be driving your car while you are away.

11.13 Keeping in touch

You may want to check if you can disconnect your home phone service and then reconnect (to your old telephone number) after your return. If you have a business phone number, you may want to consider having it route automatically to voicemail. Either way, give serious thought to bringing a good, light laptop with you on sabbatical. This will allow you to keep in touch via e-mail and Internet phone from virtually anywhere that offered wired or wireless Internet service.

11.14 Packing

Two of the biggest mistakes most inexperienced travelers make are packing too much, and not bringing what is really necessary. I have traveled to over thirty countries and lived in several, and each time I end up taking along less and less. I highly recommend visiting http://www.travelite.org for good tips on what to bring and what not to. This excellent guidance aside, the important thing to remember is that the answer for what exactly you need to bring depends upon your circumstances, where you are going, what you will be doing.

First, do you, or any family members going on sabbatical with you, have any special medical needs? Bring critical medical equipment, supplies, and also arrange to have an advance supply of any prescriptions you may be taking (actually, one year's supply would be a good idea – you cannot be sure that wherever you are going can fill these prescriptions easily if they had to). What about significant emotional needs? Children traveling with you might want to bring along a few of their most treasured toys, dolls, or books to help them feel comfortable in a new environment (but don't go overboard). If you or your partner has an important hobby or need, remember that when packing. Consider the following:

- Where are you going and what do you plan to do there?
- Are you staying in your own country? You won't need to worry about appliances not working without converters, for example.
- Will you be in one place, or traveling to many? Traveling lightly becomes even more critical in the latter case – though you may need extra equipment or maps.
- Are you planning to engage in adventure or other sporting activities?
- Will you be working?

- Which supplies and equipment will you need? Do you really need to bring them along, or can you rent these at your destination?
- What type of accommodations are you planning on staying in? Are they fully furnished, "just bring your toothbrush!" If not, how much do you need to bring and how much can you rent or buy in your destination?
- What is the climate in your destination? Pack your clothing accordingly!

Remember that if you plan to ship things or travel with extra luggage to one or more destinations and back, there is a cost associated with that. Often it is cheaper to purchase economical or second-hand items at your destination. Also, packing too many clothes, too many toiletries, a complete toolkit (aside from a handy multi-tool) and other easy-to-obtain supplies is a novice traveler's mistake.

You may need to fill out a change-of-address card to forward mail (unless someone will check up on your mail at hour home), stop subscriptions to newspapers and periodicals, arrange for movers and storage, and make final flight and lodging arrangements. Also make sure to photocopy important documents, and store away the originals.

11.15 Paperwork

Generally, it is not a good idea to bring originals of your important documents (except passports, important licenses, and other identification) with you. Instead, keep these at home, with relatives, or in a safe deposit box in a safe and fireproof location.

However, for official purposes, working, establishing a residence, establishing a bank account, and so on, it will be extremely useful to have copies (preferably notarized) of the following:

- Passports
- Birth certificates
- Marriage certificate
- Divorce certificate
- Adoption or guardianship papers
- Driver's license
- Passport-sized photographs
- Immigration documents

- Adoption papers
- Child-custody papers
- Medical insurance
- Credit cards (including credit card numbers, expiration dates, name on the card, and customer-service or loss-report phone numbers)
- Employment contract and letter of introduction (for employment arranged during a working sabbatical)
- Acceptance letter into an educational program (for an educational sabbatical)
- Medical records, including records of immunizations (critical for school-age children) and copies of any critical test results such as x-rays
- School transcripts and records (including latest report cards and assessments of any special needs or issues)
- Dental records
- Property and other insurance records
- Income tax records
- Wills
- Powers of attorney
- Lease/rental agreements
- Proofs of purchase or receipts for any high-value items you are taking with you
- Contact information/your address book (include contact information for relatives, doctors, lawyers, accountants, and anyone involved in maintaining your home while away, and make sure to leave your own contact information with key relatives, those looking after your house/tenants)

For an added measure of safety and availability, consider scanning this information electronically and sending a copy to yourself in a Web-based e-mail program (such as http://www.hotmail.com or http://www.yahoo.com). This will ensure you have access to the document anywhere with an Internet connection. If you use a PDA or mobile phone with this feature, you can store your entire address book electronically where it is easily accessible.

11.16 Health care

11.16.1 PRE-TRIP IMMUNIZATIONS AND PRESCRIPTIONS

Traveling to and within many countries requires attention to health care issues you may not normally consider at home. For example, which diseases and health conditions are typical in your destination? At least six to eight weeks before your departure schedule a visit to your physician to discuss what immunizations and medications you may need. Bring a list of possible or planned destinations and discuss any current health-care issues or medications with your doctor. You can also read up on overseas health-care issues on the U.S. Center for Disease Control's (CDC) Web site (http://www.cdc.gov/travel). Equivalent sites for the U.K. and Canada are:

> http://www.open.gov.uk/doh/hat/hatcvr.htm and
> http://www.hc-sc.ca/hpb.

You may also want to consider how you will refill any prescriptions you are now taking on an ongoing basis while you are traveling. You may be able to refill some prescriptions overseas, but others may be more complicated and require some advanced planning. If you wear glasses or contact lenses, consider bringing along multiple pairs (and a copy of your prescription and your eye doctor's contact information) as well as leaving extras with a friend who can send them if you need them. You should also order "allergy bracelets" for everyone going on sabbatical with you; these bracelets, available through Medic Alert in the U.S., list the allergies you have on an easily-identifiable bracelet.

11.16.2 MEDICAL ISSUES

Have a checkup before going on sabbatical, and get a medical opinion on whether there are any issues you should consider regarding your sabbatical – particularly if you or any family members have a chronic or special condition, or a disability. Make sure to have health insurance, and make sure it will cover you wherever you go on sabbatical. Be sure to understand the limits of your coverage.

11.16.3 HEALTH AND TRAVEL INSURANCE

Will your health plan provide full coverage of normal medical and dental expenses for you and your dependants while you are out of the country? Check your plan to see which medical expenses are covered in your sabbatical location, and whether there are any time limits beyond which coverage while you are away will lapse. If your current plan will not provide coverage, you should begin looking into local coverage you can acquire at your sabbatical destination. And the time to start looking into this is before your sabbatical!

Many policies do not cover medical evacuation for accidents suffered while traveling, or "air ambulance" services – which is why supplemental travel insurance is so popular. Many different "travel insurance" plans cover loss of luggage, trip cancellation, and some minor health-care issues. But if you are traveling for six months or more, most standard health insurance policies will not cover you, and you would be best served by some form of extended or expatriate medical coverage. The level and type of coverage will vary with your age, current health, travel style, destinations, as well as other factors. Just be sure to find a plan that provides for a significant policy maximum (at least $500,000), medical evacuation, and emergency reunion if you plan to be far from home, and your family. Several Web sites offer policy "calculators" and comparison charts including:

> http://www.lonelyplanet.com,
> http://www.travelguard.com, and
> http://www.globaltravelinsurance.com.

In either case, understand how reimbursements and claims work as it may be different for your stay away. How are claims submitted, how much is reimbursed, and amounts of co-payments and deductibles, etc.? Also, understand whether the purpose of your stay away (vacation, business, medical, etc.) will impact your coverage. Finally, you may need to let your insurance carrier know when you are leaving on sabbatical and when you are returning if this information is significant to your policy.

11.17 Schools

Some schools may not allow you to take your children out of school for a year or so for a sabbatical unless you are enrolling them in another school – they consider it "truancy." Check with your school administration early on in your sabbatical planning to see whether this would be an issue, and if so, how they suggest dealing with it.

- Do they offer any suggestions?
- Do they offer any support during the sabbatical?
- How will it affect their standing at schools?
- Would they endorse independent study/home schooling/tutoring, if you follow their curriculum and return for certain major exams?

But, if you can show that you are enrolling your children in a new school in your destination, then there is little your school could do to stand in the way.

If you arc going this route, locate a school even before you find a home. If you will be out of the country, consider whether you want a local or international school, public or private school. That decision will depend upon many factors like costs, relative quality of education, the children's language abilities, location of the school, and so on. Another option to consider is home schooling – though this will take more of your own time, and may be harder to "sell" to you child's regular school if you do not currently home-school.

11.18 Child and elder care

If you are the primary caregiver for elderly parents or relatives, you have three basic alternatives to consider:

- Having another relative or trusted friend care for them in your absence
- Placing them in an assisted-living type environment in your absence
- Taking them along with you, if their circumstances permit and if it fits with your sabbatical goals

In your sabbatical destination, you may also want to consider community or spiritual-based child or elder-care resources, if you are taking your children or parents on sabbatical with you. Other options are in-home care, provided by nannies and au-pairs. To get some ideas, here are some resources to look over:

http://www.naeyc.org,
http://www.nccic.org
http://www.aoa.dhhs.gov
http://www.caregiving.org
http://www.caremanager.org

If you share custody of your children with a divorced spouse, you need to carefully think about how these custody arrangements would work during your sabbatical. If your ex-partner agrees, you can spend more time with your children before the sabbatical and more time with them once you return. If not, think about whether you can accommodate the current custody arrangements by traveling back and forth. In many such cases, a sabbatical close to home might be a more prudent option.

11.19 Sabbatical "stuff"

Unless you are planning on staying somewhere longer than a year, the most economical way of staying at your sabbatical destination or destinations is a furnished apartment or house. Hotels of course are fine for short stays but rapidly become uneconomical. But even furnished accommodations may be missing key appliances or silverware that you need – the important thing is to be frugal in procuring these. Perhaps leasing or renting this equipment is most economical, or maybe buying second-hand things is a better option. Or – if it is cheaper to ship this from home and back than it is to buy or rent it – that may be your option. But this is more than economics – using locally acquired "things" also make your sabbatical experience more like that of a local.

If you are traveling with infants, you cannot always assume that you will find their preferred baby formula and foods at your sabbatical destination. I well remember that my daughter only drank a certain rice-based flavored formula that we were not expecting to find at our destination; I also remember the amused looks of the airport security screeners as they inspected my hand-carried 20 crates of that formula. (Ironically, the local supermarket did indeed have this formula, but how was I to know?)

If you are not driving to your sabbatical destination, then you need to consider whether you need a car where you are going. What are the costs of renting or leasing a car? How easy is it for you to drive with your current driver's license? If you need a local driver's license, how easy is it for you to convert your driver's license over? Do you need to establish residency before doing so? Or perhaps an international driving permit is acceptable. If you need a car, other alternatives to renting or leasing are shipping your car, or buying a car. Unless you are sure you will be in that location for over a year, those are probably not economical options. If you are considering shipping your car, make sure you understand the local requirements for registering and insuring it.

If you are not taking your car with you, your options are to store it, sell it, lease it, or lend it to someone you trust who can make use of it and at the same time keep it in good running condition. In such cases, both parties and a witness should sign a document of agreement. If you lease the car to someone who pays to use it, you must notify your vehicle registration authority, and register and insure it as a leased vehicle.

If your sabbatical is within driving distance, renting a U-Haul type trailer is remarkably cheap, but there are some hidden costs. It is probably best to have a heavy-duty hitch permanently installed on your car (which should be tax deductible). You should also add an additional cooling unit for the transmission if you're going any great distance. The trailer rental company can probably offer an opinion on the suitability of your car for hauling a particular sized trailer (write to the company). If you carry a trailer on your vehicle over a long distance, it is a good idea to use a trailer with a wheel size approximately equivalent to your vehicle wheels. Otherwise, you run the risk of burning out your bearings on the smaller trailer wheels if you don't keep lubricating them.

11.20 Moving and shipping

I've moved and shipped my items locally and around the world over ten times. Whether you are just moving your belongings to storage, shipping them great distances, or anything in between, the best piece of advice I can give is to select a mover based upon reputation and not just price. I and others have suffered through less-reputable movers who demand a higher price after your things are in their custody, and will not release your belongings until you pay it. I've also found things missing after a move. Check all potential movers with your local Better Business Bureau or similar, ask for references, and look more favorably upon those that have been in business for a longer time. The same holds for shipping companies, though the marketplace there is a lot smaller.

Prior to your move date, make sure to prepare any key appliances or furnishing for the move (whether or not you will be doing the packing yourself, or having the movers do it). Chandeliers need to be disconnected from their electrical source, refrigerators need to be unplugged and defrosted, and other electronics need to be properly disconnected. When moving day comes, make sure to be around. Keep an inventory list of your belongings and cross-reference these items to box or carton numbers. If you are storing some items and shipping others, you have to be extra careful to label these accordingly so they end up in the right place – and make sure your list reflects what is going where. Make sure to complete this list before the items are shipped or moved. Check your home before the movers leave to make sure nothing was left behind in closets, storage areas, attics, garages, etc. At the destination point, reconcile your packing list to the items that actually made it. Any missing items or boxes must be investigated before you pay the movers.

If you are going to ship or carry certain goods in your luggage, you are likely to have to provide the customs service of the country you are visiting with a list of these. Some of these items may not be permitted or may only be allowed with a special permit, and others may be subject to tax.

And though you may not be setting out to acquire much on your sabbatical, life is full of surprises. Souvenirs, mementos, equipment, art, supplies, and other things should be carefully thought of when planning your return. How will you bring these back? Are these duty free at source? Will you pay customs taxes at re-entry?

11.21 Booking flights

Whether you chose to do this through a travel agent or via any of the large Internet travel portals is your own choice. Just make sure to confirm your flights yourself. Also, with the flexible nature of a sabbatical, you should strive to get the most cost-effective tickets that have some flexibility with return dates (refundable tickets, or tickets with low change fees).

11.22 Travel visas

If you are a non-citizen, temporary, or permanent resident of the country and are leaving to take a sabbatical, check with your immigration authorities whether an extended stay out of the country would jeopardize your immigration standing. If so, do you need a permit to leave for your sabbatical to safeguard your status? Will you need to apply for a re-entry permit? Also remember that your precise residency status could have a significant impact on the taxes you pay in your home and sabbatical country; make sure to consult your tax advisor.

If you will be in countries other than those in which you are a citizen, it is advisable to contact the consulates to make sure there are no problems concerning leaves in those countries as long as you will not be taking paid employment while there. You will need a work visa if you are planning paid employment. In some countries, immigration may ask you to register with the local police. Allow plenty of time to get your visa and work papers. It can take anywhere from a few days to six months, depending on the country. Many nations now require much documentation to apply for a work visa, and have strict requirements for how this documentation must be authenticated. Get an early start here.

11.23 Power of attorney

From time to time you may need to be present at home for business or personal matters of a legal nature while you are on leave. Because of previous commitments, travel arrangements, or the cost involved, you may prefer to have someone act on your behalf. You can make prior arrangements for this by assigning someone power of attorney. Because this is a powerful right to delegate, consult with a lawyer before you do so. Your lawyer may also draw up a specific power of attorney form assigning an individual limited powers such as might be required in overseeing a lease agreement. In either case, however, the individual to whom you assign this power must be both responsible and trustworthy.

11.24 Internet access

Perhaps the easiest and most cost-effective means for staying in touch with friends and loved ones back home is via e-mail. Depending on your travel destinations, you may find an Internet café on every corner or go several days or weeks without seeing one. Using a travel community Web site such as those listed in the appendix can help. You can also query other travelers for information on Internet access in a specific locale, or check out a local city or country guide for your destination.

If you do not already have access to Web e-mail and an Internet service provider with worldwide access points (such as http://www.earthlink.com, http://www.aol.com, and others) you will want to set this up prior to your departure to ensure you can access all of your e-mail remotely from any Web-connected computer. Be sure to send your address to your friends and family so they can stay in touch.

An additional option is to set up an e-mail newsletter using free services from Topica or YahooGroups. To use these, you load up all of your friends' e-mail addresses (or send an e-mail inviting them to join the list) into the Web group, then each time you write an e-mail you can send it to everyone on your list with one or two quick clicks. Often you can upload pictures and other files such as your itinerary, hotel phone numbers, and addresses as well.

11.25 Telephone access and phone cards

Telephone access to and from many countries can be easy or difficult. For information on phone service and calling prices at your destinations check your guidebook, the local phone company, or a travel community Web site. Many of the larger international phone providers (AT&T, Sprint, British Telecom, etc.) offer prepaid phone cards or calling cards you can use from overseas. Rates and access points can vary wildly. As a result, you are not likely to find one single card or service that you can use from anywhere in the world. It is often best to scout out a local calling card or phone service once you arrive at your latest destination.

"Internet phone calling" (using a Web connection, rather than a phone line, and speaking into a computer's microphone to communicate) has become quite popular in many places and is significantly cheaper than landlines, but the quality and speed of the Internet connection can vary.

11.26 Safety procedures

Register with your embassy or high commission. This is important; otherwise the embassy cannot contact you in an emergency. Provide the embassy with a copy of your itinerary and your contact information. At the same time, understand what your host country's legal requirements for you are. In the Netherlands, for example, we had to register with the local police as "aliens." In other countries, you may have to register to vote, register with the tax authorities, and so on. The host country's consular affairs unit should provide you with these requirements.

Before traveling to a potentially unstable country or region, check with the U.S. Department of State or your country's external affairs division. They will provide you with information about the advisability of travel. Once in the country, register with the embassy and provide a full itinerary. In case of civil disorder, the embassy will try to contact you and provide information and advice on the situation. If evacuation is necessary, the embassy will contact registered citizens. In emergencies, the embassy may also assist with notifying relatives and evacuation plans. Embassies do not pay your travel costs when you are evacuated.

Should you be detained overseas, your embassy may be able to provide limited assistance, a list of reputable lawyers, contact relatives for notification and financial requests, and monitor your detention to ensure that your treatment conforms to local laws and standards.

11.27 Finding a place

There are two approaches to finding a place to live in your sabbatical location. One is to try and arrange one from home, and the other is to stay in a hotel or temporary accommodations until you locate one. A local real-estate professional can certainly help with the latter, while various relocation consultancies can help using the former approach. Note that there is a middle ground here too – you can arrange a pilot trip a couple of months prior to your sabbatical to check out the living options and start to look for a place. Relocation consultancies are often used by multinational enterprises that regularly relocate their employees abroad, and these consultancies can offer excellent advice and support; Relocation Resources International (RRI) is one leading firm.

When renting a property abroad, first look and try to understand the "local" housing market. Think about the following:

- What types of properties are available?
- Is the location acceptable?
- Is it an acceptable standard?
- Does it have adequate heating, air conditioning, plumbing, electrical connections, security features?
- Can you have the rental agreement looked at by a local lawyer?
- Who would you call if you have a problem with the property?
- Who would you call about problems with utilities (gas, electric, oil, water), appliances, plumbing, telephone, alarms, cable, etc.?
- What are the local practices with garbage collection and recycling?
- Are you near medical facilities/hospitals?
- Is it a safe location?
- Does it have access to public transportation/parking?

Check with the local police precinct, and talk to the locals and trusted friends or advisors.

12: **Do it!**

Now it's time to execute your plan. Do what you have been planning to do and enjoy every moment of it! In the beginning, take some time and "let go." Every so often, look back at your plan to make sure you are meeting your goals, and your positioning strategy. Be sure your sabbatical becomes the sort of story you want to tell on a job interview or to clients.

But don't get too wrapped up in self-analysis to the extent that you do not enjoy your sabbatical (just as someone busy photographing a new tourist site may not enjoy it themselves). Leave time for yourself. An excellent way for you to keep track of your progress and growth is to keep a diary. A diary has always been a favorite tool to promote self-awareness and share your experiences with others. Nowadays, you may want to post some experiences that you wish to share on a Web log or blog.

There will no doubt be challenges up ahead – things you haven't planned for, things you did not expect, no matter how good your plan. That's life – and that's a sabbatical. "Embrace change" will seem less a slogan and more a way of life that helps you become more flexible and stronger. Don't give up so easily.

There's not much else to say here – this is one chapter you will have to write for yourself.

13: After the Sabbatical

You've reached the end of your planned sabbatical. Did you meet your goals? How have you changed? How has your thinking changed? And here's the kicker – how have your future plans changed? Sometimes a break is all that's needed. You may be rearing to go back to your old job and life, refreshed and invigorated. Congratulations! Your sabbatical was a success. Others may not want to go back to their old life because their outlook and worldview have changed so much. Congratulations to you too on a successful sabbatical.

If in fact you are returning to your old job and life, there are a host of post-sabbatical issues to contend with. First, you will have to counter any perceptions of "a long vacation" or idleness you encounter back home. Here is where your positioning strategy will come in handy. Yes, you did take time to recharge your batteries, but you accomplished so much else too!

You will also have to get used to reprioritizing things in your life. Work, bills, day-to-day issues, family life, and friends will play a much bigger part, and you and your goals will for a time hold a lesser priority. It is important to re-establish old bonds, become current with your working environment, and so on – but that takes time and dedication. It may be an adjustment getting used to alarm clocks, commuting, and being in an office, so be ready.

Nonetheless, you cannot escape the fact that things have changed as a result of your sabbatical. Know what is different about you and your life and keep those differences that matter to you. When reprioritizing, you may assign a different balance to the things in your life. For example, let's look at two snapshots of an individual's time – one before a sabbatical and one after:

	Before	After
Work	65%	60%
Time with family	15%	15%
Time with friends	5%	5%
Entertainment	10%	5%
Religious services	5%	5%
Hobbies	–	5%
Volunteer work	–	5%

There isn't any one balance of activities that is right for everyone – but your sabbatical should have given you the time to reflect on what is important to you, and how to better balance your life. Now that it is done, allow it to help you make these changes.

If you did not have an employer-sponsored sabbatical, then you may have other issues to deal with as well. First, guard your self-esteem. This can be the first thing that suffers when having to look for a job – but do not let it. Remember how valuable your sabbatical has been, how refreshed, energetic, and eager you now are for a new opportunity. Keep in mind the skills you have acquired, the achievements you've racked up on sabbatical and the self-confidence you've gained after having done what you've done. Make sure to give forethought about how the skills you've acquired are transferable to the type of job you want to do. Let all of this come out when you are interviewing for a job and you should not be disappointed.

Next, spend some time testing the waters, understanding whether and how the job market has changed since you went on sabbatical. You do not want to be blindsided on an interview! Talk to old friends and colleagues, read the local newspapers and industry reports, and rejoin professional networks. Regale them with your stories, and ask them for their help. Has anything else changed in your family or circle of friends while you've been gone? Now that you're back, people will expect a fair amount of your time; you need to be ready for this.

If you are in a fast-changing field (not too many aren't nowadays) you may want to go one step further, and attempt to keep up with your field while you're away on sabbatical. You could do this by staying in touch with colleagues, reading industry magazines and journals, doing continuing education, and keeping your professional licenses or credentials up to date. As you get ready to return to work, use the Internet or a local library to read up on the latest developments. But as in all things, there must be balance here – this is a sabbatical, after all. Don't go overboard trying to stay on top of every development – prioritize, prioritize, prioritize!

Then again, you had plenty of time to think about what you want to do next during your sabbatical. Your interests, needs, capabilities, and values may have changed (not to mention the job market). Many including myself were very reluctant to give up the flexibility we so cherished on sabbatical; freelance and contract-type work, teaching, or tutoring, where one sets one's own hours and workload – can look immensely more attractive. Others make a reasoned decision to step off the "fast track" and accept a lower level position than the one they left – trading off money, title, and perks for time and lifestyle. If you are hankering for a change, this is as prudent a time as any to take the opportunity to try it.

At any rate, do not expect to jump immediately back into your old lifestyle – even if that's what you think you want to do. It takes time to find work, and to reconnect with people and routines. Give yourself some transition time (after all, you've budgeted for that, right?). This also means giving yourself time to get used to the workplace – and for the workplace to get used to you. If you are returning to your old job or company, you may find yourself having to prove yourself as if you were newly hired – whether or not those around you remember you. Also, be judicious about sharing your sabbatical stories with those beyond a close circle of colleagues and managers. Expect the reactions outside that circle (and at times from within) to range from support and admiration, to curiosity, to skepticism/jealousy/scorn. At any rate, realize that these reactions say as much or more about the people exhibiting them as they do about you.

Most of all, realize that this does not have to be the only sabbatical you ever take. You managed to do it once; you can certainly do it again. In fact, you surely have learned some lessons along the way that will make planning the next one even easier. "Gee, I wish I thought of this," or "I should have planned more time for this task," and so on, are the signposts of such lessons learned. Your next sabbatical will run even smoother.

14: **For Friends and Family**

My advice is simple: the best thing you can do for your dear sabbatical-planner is to try and understand why they are doing this, and to be as supportive as possible of their dreams and plans.

It is the most natural reaction in the world for you to feel disappointed and even somewhat rejected by your loved one or friend letting you know that they are taking a sabbatical. "Am I that bad that they need a break from me?" is a popular sentiment. "Are things here that horrible?" is another. If it is your child who is asking, you may feel an even wider range of emotions. If you depend upon your child for help, you may feel abandoned. If your child will be taking their children with them, you may be afraid that a special bond with your grandchildren may be broken. Whatever the case, talk to them openly about how you feel, and that way they can plan their sabbatical around this. The worst thing you can do is to keep quiet about your true feelings, and later let this spill over into resentment or anger. Explain your feelings and concerns, and give your child the chance to show you how they can deal with them.

But realize that a sabbatical is not about "running away" from problems (something you likely taught your children never to do). It is about how your child views themself and how they best fit into the world. It is also about resting and reflecting. And it is about renewal – coming back stronger. They are asking for distance and space – give it to them so they can grow.

Whether it is your friend or family member going on sabbatical, you may be afraid that you will grow apart with distance. My next piece of advice should come as no surprise – tell them how you feel! Let your friend explain how they can "plug you in" to their sabbatical experience however they feel most comfortable (keeping in touch by phone or e-mail, blogs, journals, and so on). Perhaps they would even like you to join in for part of their sabbatical by visiting or coming on an adventure with them; this would be an excellent way to develop a friendship.

Appendix: Resources

Craighead Inc. (http://www.craighead.com) is an excellent source of detailed country reports, written for relocating executives and expatriates and the human resources professionals who work with them.

http://www.travelite.org is the gold standard for information on packing lightly for serious travel.

Some travel sites include:

> http://www.frommers.com
> http://www.igougo.com
> http://www.lonelyplanet.com
> http://www.roughguides.com

Popular volunteering sites are:

> http://www.idealist.org
> http://www.vfp.org
> http://www.habitat.org/
> http://www.nase.org/
> http://www.workingtoday.org/
> http://www.iicd-volunteer.org/
> http://www.rlevansco.com/worldwide.html

Travel health and safety sites include:

> http://www.cdc.gov/travel/
> http://www.state.gov/travelandbusiness/
> http://travel.state.gov/travel/tips/health/health_1185.html

Established language schools that are always looking for native language instructors include:

> http://www.benedict-schools.com
> http://www.berlitz.com
> http://www.inlingua.com

Contract, temporary, full-time, project, and telecommuting job boards include:

http://www.4icj.com
http://www.accountemps.com
http://www.adecco.com
http://www.careermag.com
http://www.ceweekly.com
http://www.computerjobs.com
http://www.computerjobstore.com
http://www.computerweekly.com
http://www.computerwork.com
http://www.craigslist.com
http://www.datamasters.com
http://www.developers.net
http://www.dice.com
http://www.edpcs.com
http://www.efinancialcareers.com
http://www.elance.com
http://www.erecruitingonline.com
http://www.ework.com
http://www.freelance.com
http://www.freelancers.com
http://www.freelanceworkexchange.com
http://www.guru.com
http://www.hotjobs.com
http://www.ieeeusa.org/business/consultants
http://www.jobcenter.com
http://www.jobcircle.com
http://www.jobdigest.com
http://www.Jobsabroad.com
http://www.jobseekernews.com
http://www.jobw.com
http://www.jobwarehouse.com
http://www.justcjobs.com
http://www.kellyservices.com
http://www.manpower.com
http://www.mediabistro.com
http://www.monster.com
http://www.neoit.com
http://www.net-temps.com
http://www.network-careers.com
http://www.operationit.com
http://www.oxfordcorp.com
http://www.passportaccess.com
http://www.prgjobs.com

http://www.randstad.com
http://www.recruitersonline.com/
http://www.sohojobs.org
http://www.remedystaff.com
http://www.sunoasis.com
http://www.tacengineering.com
http://www.teksystems.com
http://www.telecommute-jobs.com/
http://www.tjobs.com
http://www.topechelon.com
http://www.tsrc.com
http://www.usjobboard.com
http://www.ustechjobs.net
http://www.vault.com
http://www.virtualresume.com
http://www.writersweekly.com

Excellent remote-working sites include:

http://www.gilgordon.com
http://www.jala.com

Sites for finding scholarships and other aid are:

http://finaid.org/scholarships/
http://www.findtuition.com/
http://www.brokescholar.com/
http://www.petersons.com
http://scholarships.fatomei.com/

Travelers medical assistance and information can be found at:

http://www.global/ems.com
http://www.sentex.net/~iamat (this site has a list of medical
    facilities and physicians, including languages spoken, for
    nearly every country)
http://www.intsos.com
http://www.medex.com
http://www.usassist.com

This site pinpoints the location of cyber cafes around the world:

http://www.cybercafes.com

For prepaid and mobile phone information, check these sites:

http://www.speedypin.com
http://www.telestial.com

An expatriate Web portal is:

> http://www.escapeartist.com

Sabbatical homes:

> http://www.sabbaticalhomes.com/
> http://www.intervac.com
> http://www.swapnow.com
> http://www.digsville.com
> http://www.homeexchange.com
> http://www.4homes.com
> http://www.swapnow.com
> http://www.gti-home-exchange.com
> http://www.holiswaps.com
> http://www.homelink.org.uk
> http://www.home-swap.com

Vacation rental sites:

> http://www.untours.com
> http://www.apartmentsapart.com

Endnotes

1   Hira, Ron and Hira, Anil, *Outsourcing America: What's Behind Our National Crisis and How We Can Reclaim American Jobs* (New York: AMACOM, 2005).

2   Stanley, T.J. and Danko, W.D. *The Millionaire Next Door* (New York: Pocket Books, 2002).